C# Learning

INDEX

Module - 5 : Classes and Objects

Classes
Objects
Inheritance
Polymorphism
A sample example with code

Module - 6 : Exception Handling

Try Catch Blocks
Finally and Throw Blocks
User Defined Exceptions

Module - 7 : Mega Project

- A Simple Calculator Application [Step by Step Tutorial]

Introduction

Abstract

Hey, guys! Thanks for downloading this ebook. I am sure that you are full of excitement to learn a whole new programming language C#, and this book is here to help you with everything at its disposal. This book is intended for beginners who want to have a know-how feel about programming and C# is one of the best languages for that. Any prior programming experience would always be good, and you would like to skip a few introductory modules and jump to the core or this book. Any feedbacks/suggestions are welcome.

Happy Learning!

Special Offer

You probably bought this book to learn more about programming in C# and make of it your work later, or to learn C# and build up your own personal project. Whatever the reason, you have chosen this book and I thank you greatly. Now I have a more than special offer to let you know! Imagine yourself learning C# programming from A to Z, acquiring the necessary knowledge to work in this field? Achieve all your goals and projects completely free? Yes, yes, for free! This is not a scam : let me explain to you. Amazon works in the following way; To increase the number of buyers and feedbacks, Amazon grants a promotion that allows, for a certain number of days, to have some books for free. Do you see what I mean? Imagine yourself getting ALL C#, C, C++ books and more again for free! Learn how to code without having to spend a single penny! Moreover, it has never been easier to join my Email list (Click the following link) :

https://williamrothschild.lpages.co/william-s-rothschild/ . You will automatically receive a confirmation email, because I want to be certain that you are interested. Do not worry, I will NOT send any spam and will not disclose your personal information to anyone. With your email address, I intend to share with you the dates when my books will be published AS WELL AS the dates when my books will be free. Also, I will share with you articles,update and useful informations to help you in your programming journey. Only individuals who have subscribed to my Email list will be able to benefit from this valuable information. Thanks you and see you soon!

Book Methodology

This book is intended for beginners having no prior programming experience. Thou, some amount of fundamental understanding will be helpful.

As described in the Index, this book is divided into several modules. Module - 1 discusses the Language C# in depth, its features, environment, IDE used and so on. Module - 2 describes the basics of any programming language keeping in mind C# as the focus and explains various data types, variables, constants, loop statements and other such things in depth with a code example on every topic. Module - 3 is all about list, strings and arrays where you can experiment with different functions and remember, these basics will be of immense help in later stages. Module - 4 discusses various loop statements, which are also equally important. Module - 5 is when we start to dive into the language by experimenting with various examples and get to know about classes and objects and how we can use them in a real-life example.

Module - 1 : Knowing C# Inside Out

Introduction to C#

C#(pronounced *see sharp*) is simple, general purpose, multi-paradigm programming language, having strong typing, object-oriented programming disciplines.

It was developed by Microsoft. Microsoft defines C# as "simple, modern, object-oriented, and typesafe programming language derived from C and C++."

C# was designed as a part of Microsoft's .Net Initiative under the leadership of Anders Hejlsberg.

There is a Rapid Application Development(RAD) protocol in C#, which means that code can be developed efficiently and fast with keywords like statement, operator, enumeration, class and structure.

If this is all sounding a little blurry, don't worry. We will be going through each of the topic in detail in the upcoming modules.

Just keep in mind that C# is CASE-SENSITIVE.

Features

C# hosts diverse features and it is known for its simplicity. C# was developed keeping in mind the combination of the best features of both the C Language and C++. It is designed for CLI - Common Language Interface which has executable code and the environment(runtime) that allows use of varied higher level languages on different computers and operating system consisting of different architectures.

A list of the primary characteristics of C#:

Object Oriented
Simple and Modern
Easy to learn
Component Oriented
Memory Management is Automatic
TypeSafe
Interoperability - Cross Platform
Structures
Part of .Net Framework

- Automatic Garbage Collection

Environment

Before starting your first C# application, one should have a look at the C# editors available for creating applications. Visual Studio .NET (VS.NET) Integrated Development Environment (IDE) is presently one of the best tools for developing C# applications. Installing VS .NET also installs the C# command-line compiler that comes with the .NET Software Development Kit (SDK).

You can install the C# command-line compiler by installing the .NET SDK. After installing the .NET SDK, you can use any C# editor.

Visual Studio 2005 Express is a lighter version of Visual Studio that is free to download. You can also download Visual C# 2005 Express version for free. To download these Express versions, go to MSDN website, select Downloads tab, and then select Visual Studio related link.

Tip: There are many C# editors available- some are even free. Many of the editors that use the C# command-line compiler are provided with the .NET SDK. You can also use any of the online C# computing environment. Whichever works best for you!

If you cannot get one of these editors, you can use a text editor, like Notepad. I would strongly recommend using the Notepad++

Your First C# Program

Well, this is it. Your first C# program. It is time for you to get your hands dirty and get onto developing code. Let's write our first simple "Hello, World!" program. The program will print output on your console saying, "Yes! I am going to learn C#!"

As mentioned earlier, if you do not have any IDE running, it is okay to write the code in a simple notepad and then saving it as "test.cs" or whatever name you want to save and keep the extension as .cs

Refer this official document for setting up the IDE or for help in running the code through command prompt - Getting Started - MSDN

Code:

```
using System;
class Hello
{
        static void Main()
        {
                Console.WriteLine("Yes! I am going to learn C#!");
        }
}
```

For compiling a C# code from the command line use the following syntax:

```
csc C:\\temp\test.cs
```

csc followed by the path where you saved your .cs le.
If your code doesn't have any errors, it successfully compiles

and produces a .exe le. Now in command prompt use the following syntax to run the program:

```
test
```

Just the lename. That's it.

Voila! It's as simple as it looks.

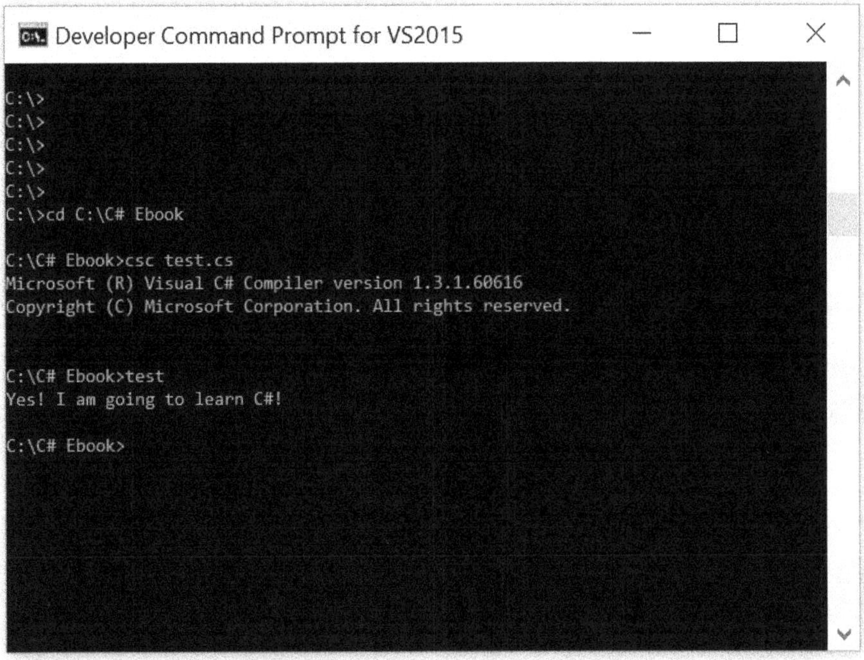
Developer Command Prompt for VS2015
C:\>
C:\>
C:\>
C:\>
C:\>
C:\>cd C:\C# Ebook
C:\C# Ebook>csc test.cs
Microsoft (R) Visual C# Compiler version 1.3.1.60616
Copyright (C) Microsoft Corporation. All rights reserved.
C:\C# Ebook>test
Yes! I am going to learn C#!
C:\C# Ebook>

You have now written your first few lines of C# code. But what does each line of your program means? I'll describe the various components of your program in the next section.

Module - 2 : Getting The Basics Right

Data Types

Since you are now familiar with writing C# code, we will now focus on the data types, variables, operators, etc. To be specific, you will learn how to name, declare and initialize data types and stuff.

C# Variables are mainly of the following three types:

1. Value Types
2. Reference Types
3. Pointer Types

Value types includes simple data types like int, char, and bool. Reference types includes object, class, interface, and delegates.

A value type contains the actual value of the object. That means the actual data is stored in the variable of a value type, whereas a reference type variable contains the reference to the actual data.

1) Value Types:

These types can be assigned a value directly. Class used is : System.ValueType. They directly have/contain the data. Int, char, oat, bool, decimal are some of the examples of value types. For example, when an int variable is declared, system automatically allocates the memory to store the value.

The table below explains the various value types and its size and characteristics.

Type	Description	Range	Default Value
bool	Boolean value	True or False	False
Type	Description	Range	Default Value
byte	8-bit unsigned integer	0 to 255	0
har	16-bit Unicode character	U +0000 to U +ffff	'\0'
decimal	128-bit precise decimal values with 28-29 signi cant digits	(-7.9 x 1028 to 7.9 x 1028) / 100 to 28	0.0M
double	64-bit double-precision oating point type	(+/-)5.0 x 10-324 to (+/-)1.7 x 10308	0.0D
oat	32-bit single-precision oating point type	-3.4 x 1038 to + 3.4 x 1038	0.0F
int	32-bit signed integer type	-2,147,483,648 to 2,147,483,647	0
long	64-bit signed	- 9,223,372,036,854,	0L

	integer type	775,808 to 9,223,372,036,854, 775,807	
Type	Description	Range	Default Value
sbyte	8-bit signed integer type	-128 to 127	0
short	16-bit signed integer type	-32,768 to 32,767	0
uint	32-bit unsigned integer type	0 to 4,294,967,295	0
ulong	64-bit unsigned integer type	0 to 18,446,744,073,709 ,551,615	0
ushort	16-bit unsigned integer type	0 to 65,535	0

You may have a better understanding once you go through this program. You are free to experiment with this code and try to dive in as much as possible using the information in the table.

Code:

```
Using System; namespace
ToStringSamp

{

class Test

{

        static void Main(string[ ] args)

        {

                int num 1 =12; float
                num2 =3.05f; double
                num3 = 3.5; bool bl =
                true;
                Console.WriteLine(num1.ToString());
                Console. WriteLine(num2.ToString());
                Console.WriteLine(bl.ToString());


        }

}

}
```

Output:

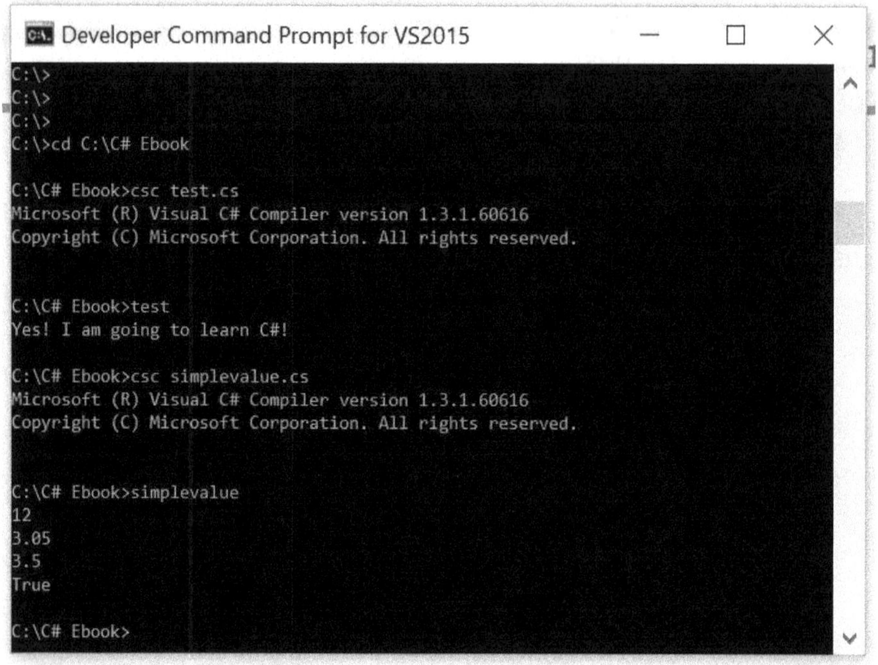

Developer Command Prompt for VS2015
C:\>
C:\>
C:\>
C:\>cd C:\C# Ebook
C:\C# Ebook>csc test.cs
Microsoft (R) Visual C# Compiler version 1.3.1.60616
Copyright (C) Microsoft Corporation. All rights reserved.
C:\C# Ebook>test
Yes! I am going to learn C#!
C:\C# Ebook>csc simplevalue.cs
Microsoft (R) Visual C# Compiler version 1.3.1.60616
Copyright (C) Microsoft Corporation. All rights reserved.
C:\C# Ebook>simplevalue
12
3.05
3.5
True
C:\C# Ebook>

2) Reference Types:

A reference type is a reference to an instance type. The main reference types are class, array, interface, delegate, and event. A null value is assigned to a reference type by default. A type assigned to a null value means the absence of an instance of that type. We will go into this in detail in upcoming modules.

3) Pointer Types:

In Pointer type variables store the memory address of another type. It is same as in C and C++.

Syntax for declaring is :

```
type* identifier;
```

Example:

float* fptr;

int* iptr;

Variables

A variable is a name given to a storage area that the programs can manipulate. Each variable in C# has a specific type, which can determine the size and layout of the variable's memory, the range of values that can be stored within that memory and the set of operations that can be applied to the variable.
The basic value types provided in C# are given as below:

Type	Example
Integral types	sbyte, byte, short, ushort, int, uint, long, ulong, and char
Floating point types	oat and double
Decimal types	decimal
Boolean types	true or false values, as assigned
Nullable types	Nullable data types

Constants

Constants are similar to read-only fields. You can't change a constant value once it's assigned. The const keyword precedes the field to define it as a constant. Assigning value to a constant would give a compilation error.

Syntax:

```
const <data_type> <constant_name> = value;
```

Example:

```
const double pi = 3.14159;
```

Expressions and Operators

An expression is a sequence of operators and operands that specify some sort of computation. The operators indicate an operation to be applied to one or two operands. For example, the operators + and - indicate adding and subtracting operands. For example, the operator + and - indicate adding and subtracting one object from another, respectively.

An operator is just a symbol that tells the compiler what type of computation is required. C# has a rich set of built - in operators like:

Arithmetic Operators
Relational Operators
Logical Operators
Bitwise Operators
Assignment Operators
Misc Operators

ARITHMETIC OPERATORS

Operator	Description	Example
+	Adds two operands	A + B = 30
-	Subtracts second operand from the first	A - B = -10
*	Multiplies both operands	A * B = 200
/	Divides numerator by denominator	B / A = 2
%	Modulus Operator and remainder of after an integer division	B % A = 0
++	Increment operator increases integer value by one	A++ = 11
--	Decrement operator decreases integer value by one	A-- = 9

RELATIONAL OPERATORS

Operator	Description	Example
==	Checks if the values of two operands are equal or not, if yes then condition becomes true.	(A == B) is not true.
!=	Checks if the values of two operands are equal or not, if values are not equal then condition becomes true.	(A != B) is true.
>	Checks if the value of left operand is greater than the value of right operand, if yes then condition becomes true.	(A > B) is not true.
<	Checks if the value of left operand is less than the value of right operand, if yes then condition becomes true.	(A < B) is true.
>=	Checks if the value of left operand is greater than or equal to the value of right operand, if yes then condition becomes true.	(A >= B) is not true.
<=	Checks if the value of left operand is less than or equal to the value of right operand, if yes then condition becomes true.	(A <= B) is true.

LOGICAL OPERATORS

Operator	Description	Example
&&	Called Logical AND operator. If both the operands are non zero then condition becomes true.	(A && B) is false.
||	Called Logical OR Operator. If any of the two operands is non zero then condition becomes true.	(A || B) is true.
!	Called Logical NOT Operator. Use to reverses the logical state of its operand. If a condition is true then Logical NOT operator will make false.	!(A && B) is true.

BITWISE OPERATORS

p	q	p & q	p | q	p ^ q
0	0	0	0	0
0	1	0	1	1
1	1	1	1	0
1	0	0	1	1

ASSIGNMENT OPERATORS

Operator	Description	Example
=	Simple assignment operator, Assigns values from right side operands to left side operand	C = A + B assigns value of A + B into C
+=	Add AND assignment operator, It adds right operand to the left operand and assign the result to left operand	C += A is equivalent to C = C + A
-=	Subtract AND assignment operator, It subtracts right operand from the left operand and assign the result to left operand	C -= A is equivalent to C = C - A
*=	Multiply AND assignment operator, It multiplies right operand with the left operand and assign the result to left operand	C *= A is equivalent to C = C * A
/=	Divide AND assignment operator, It divides left operand with the right operand and assign the result to left operand	C /= A is equivalent to C = C / A
%=	Modulus AND assignment operator, It takes modulus using	C %= A is

	two operands and assign the result to left operand	equivalent to C = C % A
<<=	Left shift AND assignment operator	C <<= 2 is same as C = C << 2
>>=	Right shift AND assignment operator	C >>= 2 is same as C = C >> 2
&=	Bitwise AND assignment operator	C &= 2 is same as C = C & 2
^=	bitwise exclusive OR and assignment operator	C ^= 2 is same as C = C ^ 2
|=	bitwise inclusive OR and assignment operator	C |= 2 is same as C = C | 2

OTHER OPERATORS

Operator	Description	Example
sizeof()	Returns the size of a data type.	sizeof(int), returns 4.
typeof()	Returns the type of a class.	typeof(StreamReader);
&	Returns the address of a variable.	&a; returns actual address of the variable.
*	Pointer to a variable.	*a; creates pointer named 'a' to a variable.
? :	Conditional Expression	If Condition is true ? Then value X : Otherwise value Y

is	Determines whether an object is of
	a certain type.
		If(Ford is Car) // checks if Ford is an
		object of the Car class.

as	Cast without raising an exception if the cast fails.	Object obj = new StringReader("Hello"); StringReader r = obj as StringReader;

Type Casting

Type casting is a way of converting from one data type to another. For an example, if we want an integer, but the data type is float or double, we can easily convert this to int with the help of type casting.

To convert one numeric data type to another, we just need to add (new data type) in front of the data that we want to convert.

Example:

Int x = (int) 12.345;

Now, this stores the value of x as 12, after casting the 12.345 value into an integer value. Decimal portion gets trimmed off after conversion. Some other types of casting are also available. We discuss these in the modules to come.

Module - 3 : Arrays, Lists and Strings

Array and it's Methods

An array is a sequential set of elements of one(same) data type. An array is said to be a collection of similar data types, which has a contiguous memory allocation. Arrays are of two kinds, single-dimensional array and multi-dimensional array. There is a term jagged-arrays simply meaning array inside an array. We will get into that later. An array always starts with it's lower index by 0. The upper index is number of items minus 1.

You can initialize array item either during the creation of an array or later by referencing array item, as shown here:

int[] nums = new int[5];

int[0] = 1;

int[1] = 2;

int[2] = 3;

int[3] = 4;

int[4] = 5;

You can also use the below mentioned method for an array declaration:

int[] nums = new int {1,2,3,4,5,};

Syntax for declaring arrays:

To declare an array, we use the following syntax:

```
datatype[] arrayName;
```

Example:

Int[] sum;

Syntax for initialising arrays:

When we declare an array, it is not automatically initialized. Initializing means creation of an instance of that particular array object. We use the new keyword for initializing the array like this:

```
int[] sum= new int[10];
```

Code:

```
class Test

{

static void Main()

{

//array of integers

int[] nums = new int[5];

// Array of strings

string[ ] names = new string[2];

for(int i =0; i< nums.Length; i++)
nums[i] = i+2;
```

```
names[0] = "John";

names[1] = "Mayor";

for (int i = 0; i< nums.Length; i++)

System.Console.WriteLine ("num[{0}] = {1}", i, nums[i] );

System.Console.WriteLine

(names[0].ToString() + " " + names[1].ToString() );

}

}
```

Output:

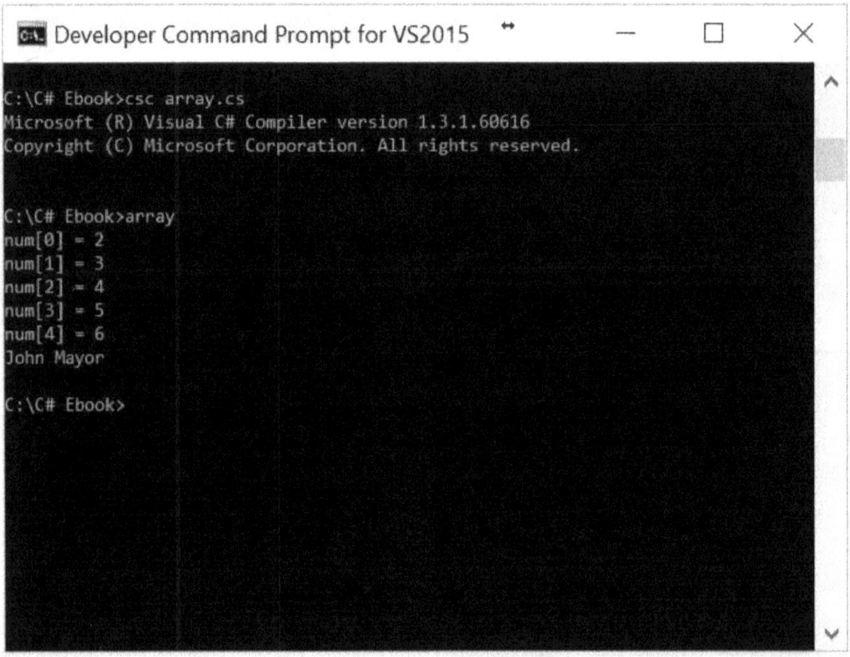
Developer Command Prompt for VS2015
C:\C# Ebook>csc array.cs
Microsoft (R) Visual C# Compiler version 1.3.1.60616
Copyright (C) Microsoft Corporation. All rights reserved.
C:\C# Ebook>array
num[0] = 2
num[1] = 3
num[2] = 4
num[3] = 5
num[4] = 6
John Mayor
C:\C# Ebook>

You might have noticed that in the code, there are fragments which you might not have understood, like the for loops. For beginners, don't worry, we have a separate module for the loops further ahead in this book.

This might be relatively easy to catch up for those having a preliminary touch of looping statements in any other programming languages. It is the same in C#. Do not worry, in any case we will be covering the loops in the next module.

Array Methods:

Length:

Returns an integer value of length of array.
Example:

```
int i = arr1.Length;
```

Rank:

Returns integer value of total number items in all dimensions.

Example:

```
int i = arr1.Rank;
```

isFixedSize:

Returns boolean value of whether array is fixed size or not.

Example:

```
bool i = arr.IsFixedSize;
```

isReadOnly:
Returns boolean value of whether array is read only or not.

Example:

```
bool k = arr1.IsReadOnly;
```

Function	Explanation	Example
Sort	Sorting an array	Array.Sort(arr1);
Clear	Clearing an array	Array.Clear(arr1,0,2);
GetLength	Return Number of elements	arr1.GetLength(0);
GetValue	Return's value of particular items	arr1.GetValue(2);
Copy	Copy all the array elements	Array.copy(arr1,arr2,3);
IndexOf	Returns the index position of value	Array.IndexOf(arr1,45);

Code:

```
using System;

class Program

{
```

```
        static void Main()

        {

            string[] array = { "A", "B", "C", "D" };


            // The "A" string is at index 1.
            Int AIndex = Array.IndexOff(array, "A");
            Console.WriteLine(Aindex);

            // There is no "E" string in the array.

            // ... So IndexOf returns -1.
            int EIndex = Array.IndexOf(array, "E");
            Console.WriteLine(EIndex);

        // Create string array with no elements. var empty1 = new
string[] { }; Console.WriteLine(empty1.Length == 0);

// This syntax has the same result. var empty2 =
new string[0]; Console.WriteLine(empty2.Length
 == 0);

        // Get the last string element.
Console.WriteLine(array[array.Length - 1]);

        string first = array[0];
        Console.WriteLine(first);

        }
}
```

Output:

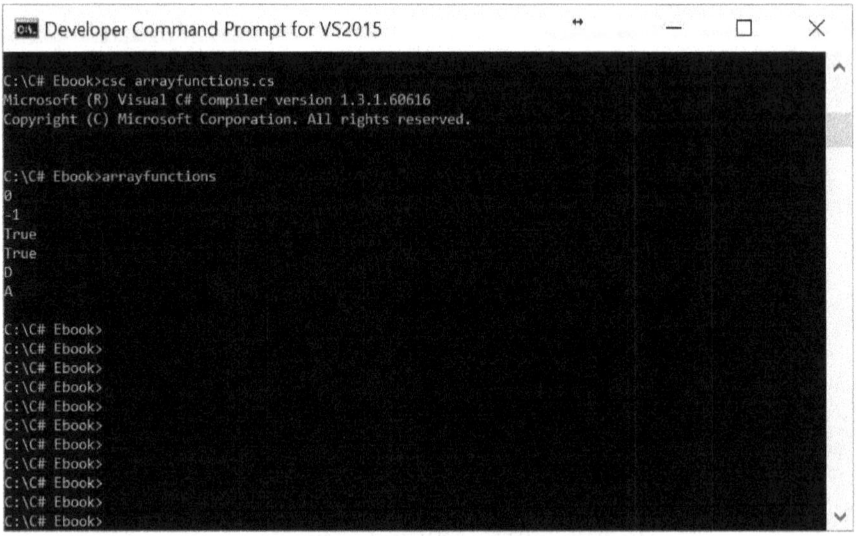
Developer Command Prompt for VS2015
C:\C# Ebook>csc arrayfunctions.cs
Microsoft (R) Visual C# Compiler version 1.3.1.60616
Copyright (C) Microsoft Corporation. All rights reserved.
C:\C# Ebook>arrayfunctions
0
-1
True
True
D
A
C:\C# Ebook>
C:\C# Ebook>
C:\C# Ebook>
C:\C# Ebook>
C:\C# Ebook>
C:\C# Ebook>
C:\C# Ebook>
C:\C# Ebook>
C:\C# Ebook>
C:\C# Ebook>
C:\C# Ebook>

This example showed some of the array functions, and I encourage you to try out the rest of the mentioned array functions from the table given above on your own.

Lists and it's Methods

In literal terms, a list can be defined as a generic list of items. List can be of any type. It can either be reference type or value type as per the need.

```
var list1 = new List<object>();

var list2 = new List<buyer>();

var list3 = new List<int>();
```

New records are joined at the end of the list. A list is first initialised and then it adjusts the size as required automatically.

We can easily create an empty list by using the following syntax:

```
var list = new List<int>();
```

Creating and initialising the list with numerical entries:

```
var list = new List<int>() { 10, 5, 2 };
```

Creating a list and initialising it with values of another list:

```
var listA = new List<int>() { 10, 5, 2 };

var listB = new List<int>(listA);
```

Here we have two lists, List A and List B having same elements inside them: {10,5,2}

Creating a list with specific limit:

```
var list = new List<int>(20);
```

Here is a simple C# program for adding elements and displaying in the list.

Code:

```
usingSystem.collections.Generic; class
Program

{

        static void Main()

        {
                List<int>list= new List<int>(); list.Add(2);

                list.Add(3);

                list.Add(7);

                //Loop through List with foreach.foreach (int

                Prime in list)

                {

                        System.Console.WriteLine(prime);

                }

        }

}
```

Output:

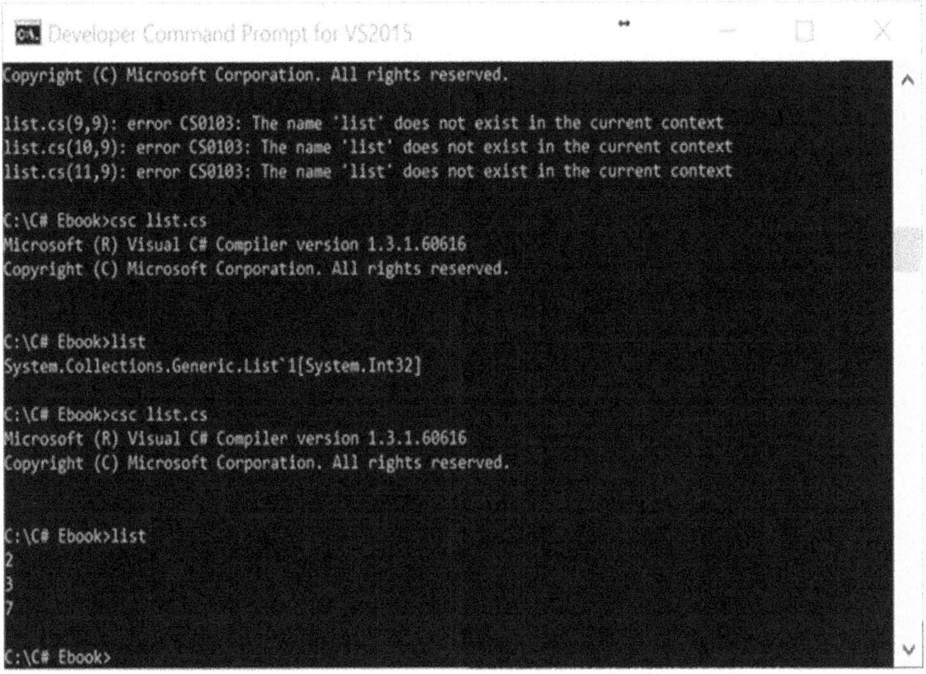
Developer Command Prompt for VS2015
Copyright (C) Microsoft Corporation. All rights reserved.
list.cs(9,9): error CS0103: The name 'list' does not exist in the current context
list.cs(10,9): error CS0103: The name 'list' does not exist in the current context
list.cs(11,9): error CS0103: The name 'list' does not exist in the current context
C:\C# Ebook>csc list.cs
Microsoft (R) Visual C# Compiler version 1.3.1.60616
Copyright (C) Microsoft Corporation. All rights reserved.
C:\C# Ebook>list
System.Collections.Generic.List`1[System.Int32]
C:\C# Ebook>csc list.cs
Microsoft (R) Visual C# Compiler version 1.3.1.60616
Copyright (C) Microsoft Corporation. All rights reserved.
C:\C# Ebook>list
2
3
7
C:\C# Ebook>

List Methods:

Add:

Used for adding an element at the end of the list. Example:

```
list.Add(5);
```

AddRange:

Used for adding an elements of another list at the end of the current list. Example:

```
listA.AddRange(listB);
```

Clear:

Used for removing all elements of list.

Example:

```
list.Clear();
```

Contains:

Used for checking if the element is present in the list or not. Returns true/false Example:

```
bool result = list.Contains(3);
```

ConvertAll:

Used for converting all the items to a specific another type.

Example:

```
var conv = new Converter<int,decimal>(x => (decimal)(x+1));

var listB = listA.ConvertAll<decimal>(conv);
```

This converts all the items from int to decimal.

GetRange:

Returns list of items from one
with the source list. Example:

```
var listB = listA.GetRange(index: 1, count: 3);
```

Insert:

Insert an item in the list at
a particular index. Example:

```
list.Insert(index: 1, item: 5);
```

InsertRange:

Same as AddRange.

Example:

```
listA.InsertRange(index: 1,collection: listB);
```

There are many more functions - Remove, RemoveAll, RemoveAt, RemoveRange, Reverse, Sort, Trim, etc. These are all equally important. Now that you have developed a sense of how to use these functions, feel free to experiment on your own using a test list. You can use the MSDN forum for more help on these.

Here I have demonstrated the use of some of the methods :

Counting List

Code:

```
using System;

using System.Collections.Generic;


class Program

{

        static void Main()

        {
```

```
            List<bool> list = new List<bool>();
            list.Add(true);
            list.Add(false);
            list.Add(true);

            Console.WriteLine(list.Count); // 3

            list.Clear();
            Console.WriteLine(list.Count); // 0
        }
}
```

Output:

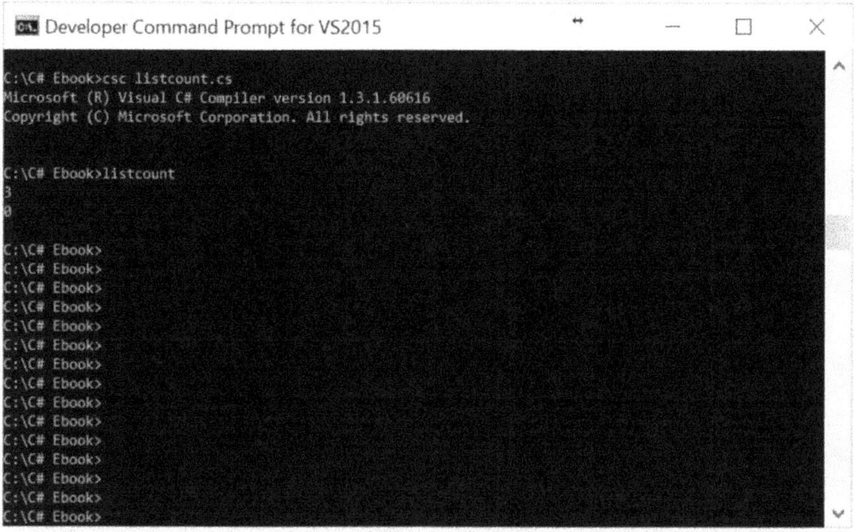
Developer Command Prompt for VS2015
C:\C# Ebook>csc listcount.cs
Microsoft (R) Visual C# Compiler version 1.3.1.60616
Copyright (C) Microsoft Corporation. All rights reserved.
C:\C# Ebook>listcount
3
0
C:\C# Ebook>
C:\C# Ebook>
C:\C# Ebook>
C:\C# Ebook>
C:\C# Ebook>
C:\C# Ebook>
C:\C# Ebook>
C:\C# Ebook>
C:\C# Ebook>
C:\C# Ebook>
C:\C# Ebook>
C:\C# Ebook>
C:\C# Ebook>
C:\C# Ebook>
C:\C# Ebook>

Copying an array

Code:

```
using System;

using System.Collections.Generic;

class Program

{

    static void Main()

    {

        int[] arr = new int[3]; // New array with 3 elements.
    arr[0] = 2;

        arr[1] = 3;
        arr[2] = 5;

        List<int> list = new List<int>(arr); // Copy to List.
```

```
            Console.WriteLine(list.Count); // 3 elements in List.

        }

}
```

Output:

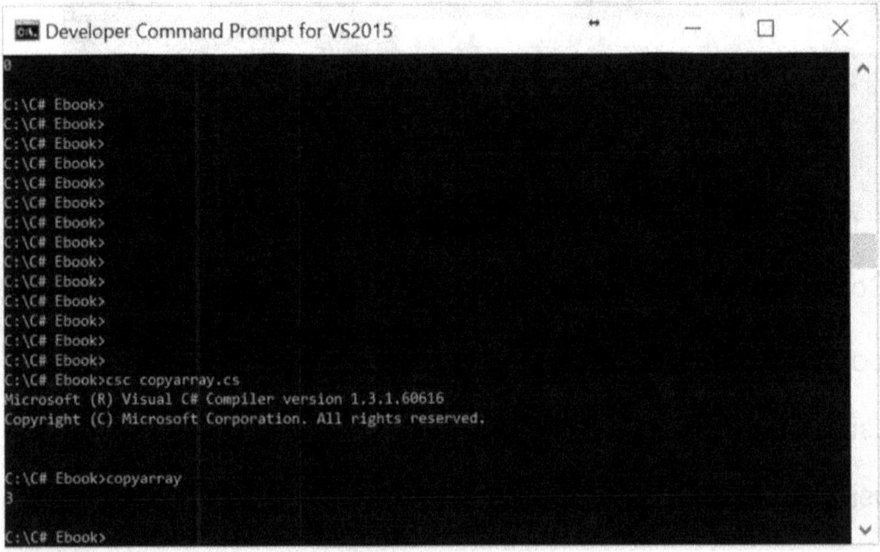
Developer Command Prompt for VS2015
0
C:\C# Ebook>
C:\C# Ebook>
C:\C# Ebook>
C:\C# Ebook>
C:\C# Ebook>
C:\C# Ebook>
C:\C# Ebook>
C:\C# Ebook>
C:\C# Ebook>
C:\C# Ebook>
C:\C# Ebook>
C:\C# Ebook>
C:\C# Ebook>
C:\C# Ebook>
C:\C# Ebook>csc copyarray.cs
Microsoft (R) Visual C# Compiler version 1.3.1.60616
Copyright (C) Microsoft Corporation. All rights reserved.
C:\C# Ebook>copyarray
3
C:\C# Ebook>

IndexOf

Code:

```
using System;

using System.Collections.Generic;

class Program

{
```

```
        static void Main()

        {

                List<int> primes = new List<int>(new int[] { 19, 23,
        29 });

                Int index = prime.IndexOf(23); // Exists.

                Console.WriteLine(index);

                Index= primes.IndexOf(10); // Does not exist.

                Console.WriteLine(index);


        }

}
```

Output:

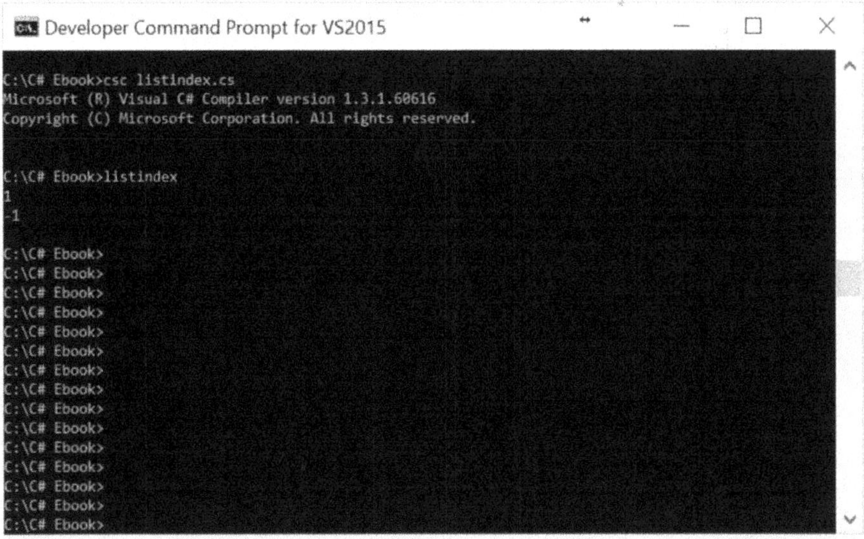
Developer Command Prompt for VS2015
C:\C# Ebook>csc listindex.cs
Microsoft (R) Visual C# Compiler version 1.3.1.60616
Copyright (C) Microsoft Corporation. All rights reserved.
C:\C# Ebook>listindex
1
-1
C:\C# Ebook>
C:\C# Ebook>
C:\C# Ebook>
C:\C# Ebook>
C:\C# Ebook>
C:\C# Ebook>
C:\C# Ebook>
C:\C# Ebook>
C:\C# Ebook>
C:\C# Ebook>
C:\C# Ebook>
C:\C# Ebook>
C:\C# Ebook>
C:\C# Ebook>
C:\C# Ebook>

Reverse

Code:

```
using System;

using System.Collections.Generic;

class Program

{

        static void Main()

        {

        List<string>list = new List<string>();

        List.Add("anchovy"); list.Add("barracuda");

        list.Add("bass"); list.Add("viperfish");


        // Reverse List in-place, no new variables required.
        list.Reverse();


        foreach (string value in list)

        {

                Console.WriteLine(value);
```

```
                }

        }

}
```

Output:

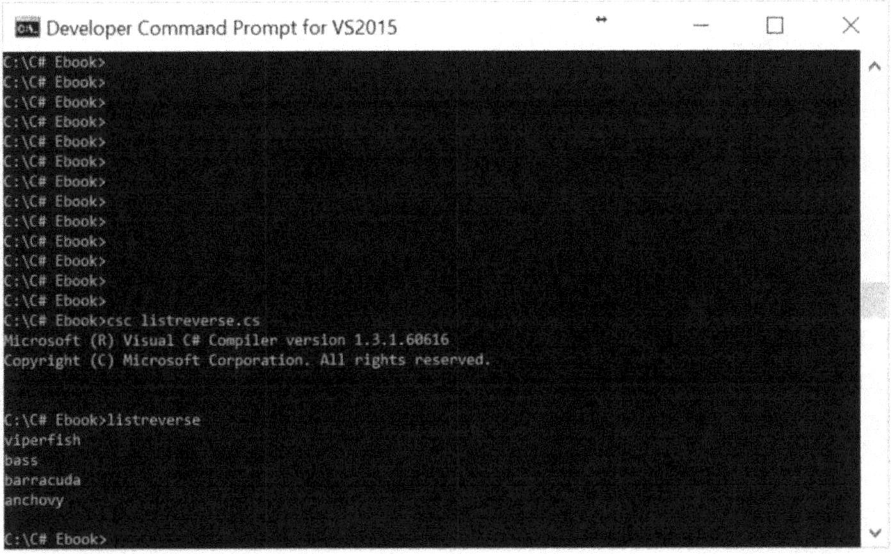
Developer Command Prompt for VS2015
C:\C# Ebook>
C:\C# Ebook>
C:\C# Ebook>
C:\C# Ebook>
C:\C# Ebook>
C:\C# Ebook>
C:\C# Ebook>
C:\C# Ebook>
C:\C# Ebook>
C:\C# Ebook>
C:\C# Ebook>
C:\C# Ebook>
C:\C# Ebook>
C:\C# Ebook>csc listreverse.cs
Microsoft (R) Visual C# Compiler version 1.3.1.60616
Copyright (C) Microsoft Corporation. All rights reserved.
C:\C# Ebook>listreverse
viperfish
bass
barracuda
anchovy
C:\C# Ebook>

String and it's Methods

Strings are nothing but array of characters. It comes under the System.String class. Strings have characters and words. There are various methods by which you can create a string variable:

Using a sting class container

By using the concatenation operator of string i.e +

Assigning a string literal to string variable, etc.

String has two properties as follows:

Chars

Length

String Methods:

Like Arrays and Lists, strings have a ton of methods. Listing some of the methods for your reference:

Compare
CompareOrdinal
CompareTo
Concat
Contains
Copy
CopyTo
EndsWith
Empty
Equals
Format
GetEnumerator
GetHashCode
IndexOf
IndexOfAny
Insert
Intern
IsInterned

IsNormalized
IsNullOrEmpty
IsNullOrWhiteSpace
Join
PadLeft
PadRight
Remove
Replace
Split
StartsWith
Substring
ToCharArray
ToLower
ToLowerInvariant
ToString
ToUpper
ToUpperInvariant
Trim
TrimEnd
TrimStart

It is out of scope of this ebook to explain all of these, but a few important ones are described below:

Compare:

This method determines the sorting order of strings. There are a total of three methods:

Compare
CompareOrdinal
CompareTo
Code:

```
using System; class Program

{
```

```
static void Main()

{

    string a = "a"; string

     b = "b";

    int c = string.Compare(a, b);

    Console.WriteLine(c);

    c = string.CompareOrdinal(b, a);

     Console.WriteLine(c);

    c = a.CompareTo(b);

    Console.WriteLine(c); c =

    b.CompareTo(a);

    Console.WriteLine(c);

}

}
```

Output:

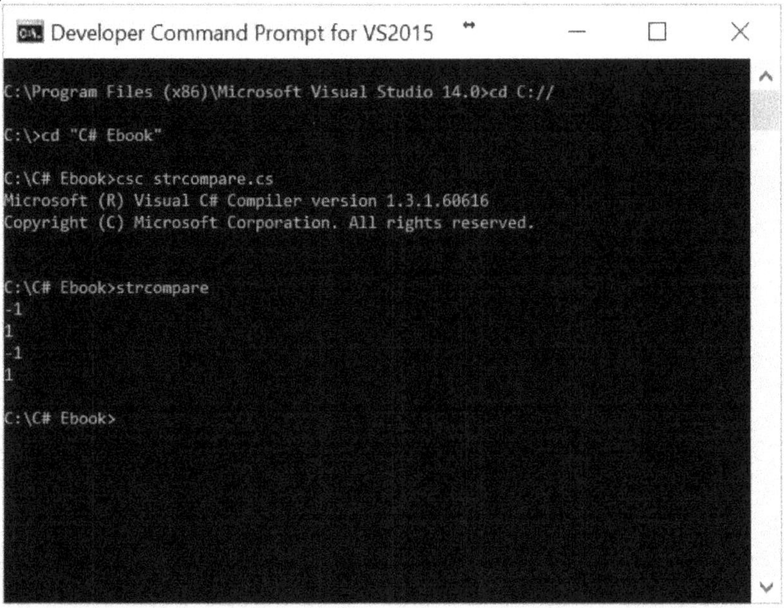
Developer Command Prompt for VS2015
C:\Program Files (x86)\Microsoft Visual Studio 14.0>cd C://
C:\>cd "C# Ebook"
C:\C# Ebook>csc strcompare.cs
Microsoft (R) Visual C# Compiler version 1.3.1.60616
Copyright (C) Microsoft Corporation. All rights reserved.
C:\C# Ebook>strcompare
-1
1
-1
1
C:\C# Ebook>

Concat:

Used for concatenation of two strings. This code snippet is going to boost you.

Code:

```
using System;
class Program

{
        static void Main()

        {

                ... Create a new string reference.
                        It points to the literal. string s1 =
        "string2";
                ... Add another string to the start. string s2 =
        "string1" + s1; Console.WriteLine(s2);

        }

}
```

Output:

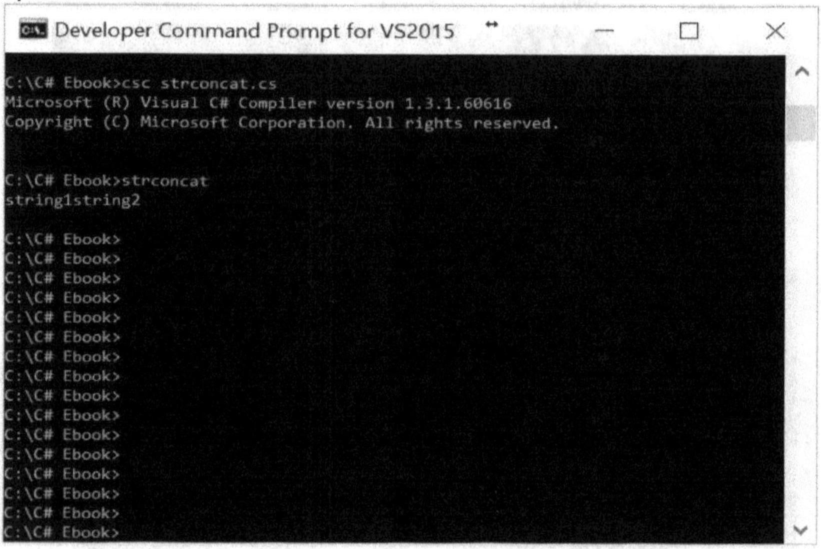
Developer Command Prompt for VS2015
C:\C# Ebook>csc strconcat.cs
Microsoft (R) Visual C# Compiler version 1.3.1.60616
Copyright (C) Microsoft Corporation. All rights reserved.
C:\C# Ebook>strconcat
string1string2
C:\C# Ebook>
C:\C# Ebook>
C:\C# Ebook>
C:\C# Ebook>
C:\C# Ebook>
C:\C# Ebook>
C:\C# Ebook>
C:\C# Ebook>
C:\C# Ebook>
C:\C# Ebook>
C:\C# Ebook>
C:\C# Ebook>
C:\C# Ebook>
C:\C# Ebook>
C:\C# Ebook>
C:\C# Ebook>

Copy:

Used for copying string data.

Code:

```
using System;

class Program
{
	static void Main()
	{
		//
		// Copy a literal string.
		//
		string value1 = "Literal";
```

```
            string value2 = string.Copy(value1);

            //
            // Write the string values.
            //
            Console.WriteLine(value1);
            Console.WriteLine(value2);

            // See if the references are equal.
            //
            Console.WriteLine(object.ReferenceEquals(value1,
            value2));
        }
}
```

Output:

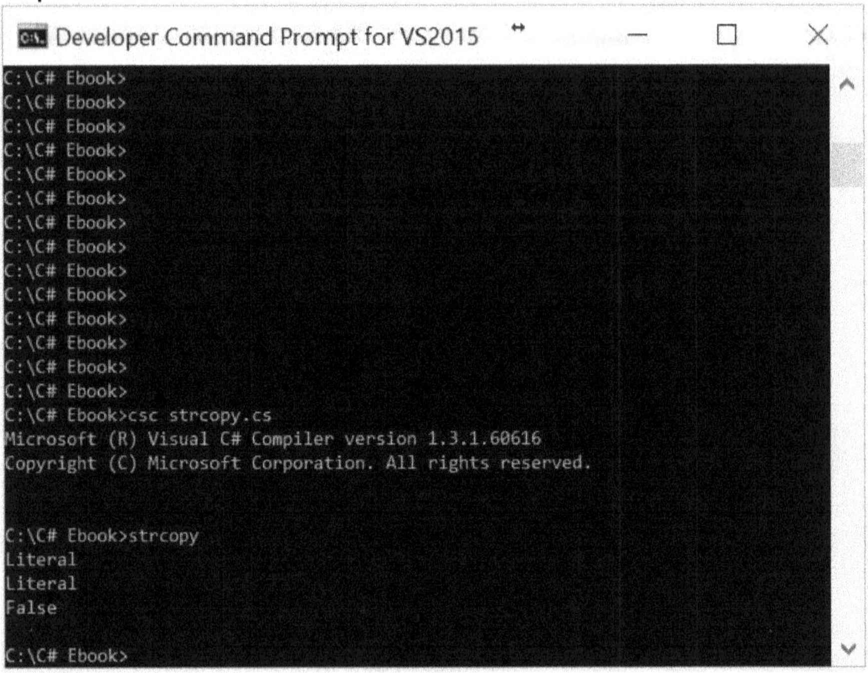
Developer Command Prompt for VS2015
C:\C# Ebook>
C:\C# Ebook>
C:\C# Ebook>
C:\C# Ebook>
C:\C# Ebook>
C:\C# Ebook>
C:\C# Ebook>
C:\C# Ebook>
C:\C# Ebook>
C:\C# Ebook>
C:\C# Ebook>
C:\C# Ebook>
C:\C# Ebook>
C:\C# Ebook>
C:\C# Ebook>csc strcopy.cs
Microsoft (R) Visual C# Compiler version 1.3.1.60616
Copyright (C) Microsoft Corporation. All rights reserved.
C:\C# Ebook>strcopy
Literal
Literal
False
C:\C# Ebook>

IndexOf:

Used to check if a string contains a specific word.

Code:

```
using System; class Program

{

        static void Main()

        {

                // The input string.

                const string value = "Your dog is cute."; // Test
        withIndexOf method.

                if (value.IndexOf("dog") != -1)
```

```
{
        Console.WriteLine("string contains dog!");
        }
}
```

Output:

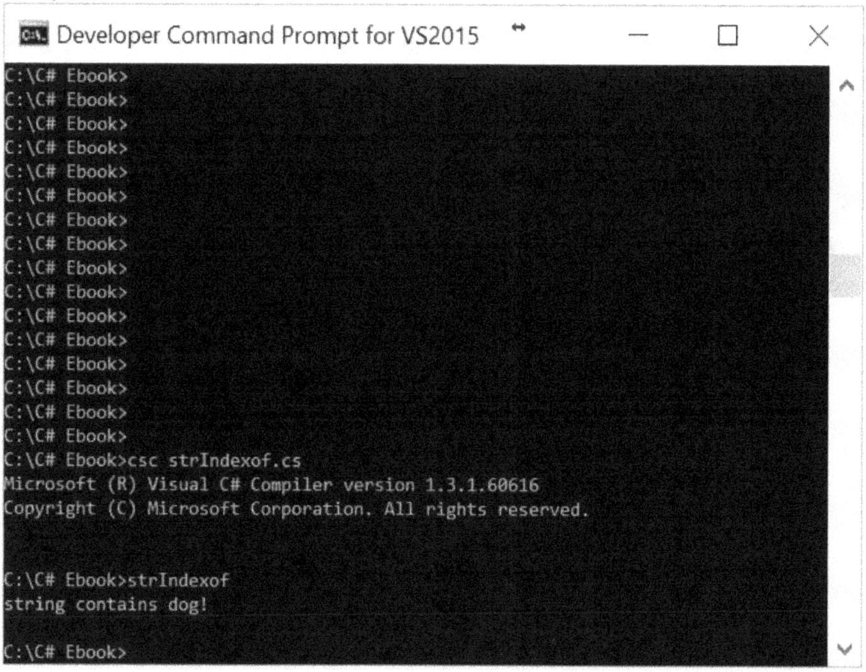
Developer Command Prompt for VS2015
C:\C# Ebook>
C:\C# Ebook>
C:\C# Ebook>
C:\C# Ebook>
C:\C# Ebook>
C:\C# Ebook>
C:\C# Ebook>
C:\C# Ebook>
C:\C# Ebook>
C:\C# Ebook>
C:\C# Ebook>
C:\C# Ebook>
C:\C# Ebook>
C:\C# Ebook>
C:\C# Ebook>
C:\C# Ebook>
C:\C# Ebook>csc strIndexof.cs
Microsoft (R) Visual C# Compiler version 1.3.1.60616
Copyright (C) Microsoft Corporation. All rights reserved.
C:\C# Ebook>strIndexof
string contains dog!
C:\C# Ebook>

LastIndexOf:

Used to search a string from the right. It is simply reversed version of IndexOf.

Code:

```
using System;


class Program

{

        static void Main()

        {

                //

                        The string we are searching. string

           value = "Dot Net Test";

                        Find the last occurrence of N. int index1 =

           value.LastIndexOf('N'); if (index1 != -1)

        {

                Console.WriteLine(index1);

                Console.WriteLine(value.Substring(index1));

}

                Find the last occurrence of this string. Int index2 =

           value.LastIndexOf("Test");

                if (index2 != -1)

        {
```

```
            Console.WriteLine(index2);
            Console.WriteLine(value.Substring(index2));
        }
        //
        // Find the last 'e'.
        // ... This will not find the first 'e'. int index3 =
        value.LastIndexOf('e');
        if (index3 != -1)
        {
            Console.WriteLine(index3);
            Console.WriteLine(value.Substring(index3));
        }
            int index4 = value.LastIndexOf("Test",
                StringComparison.OrdinalIgnoreCase);
            if (index4 != -1)
        {
            Console.WriteLine(index4);
            Console.WriteLine(value.Substring(index4));
            }
        }
}
```

Output:

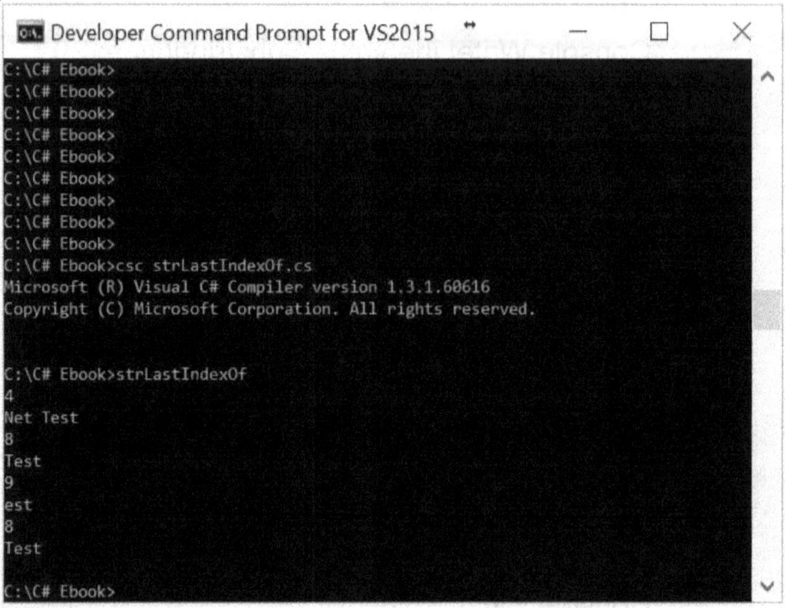
Developer Command Prompt for VS2015
C:\C# Ebook>
C:\C# Ebook>
C:\C# Ebook>
C:\C# Ebook>
C:\C# Ebook>
C:\C# Ebook>
C:\C# Ebook>
C:\C# Ebook>
C:\C# Ebook>
C:\C# Ebook>csc strLastIndexOf.cs
Microsoft (R) Visual C# Compiler version 1.3.1.60616
Copyright (C) Microsoft Corporation. All rights reserved.
C:\C# Ebook>strLastIndexOf
4
Net Test
8
Test
9
est
8
Test
C:\C# Ebook>

Trim:

This method trims the left and right white spaces.

Code:

```
using System;

class Program

{

        static void Main()

        {

                // Input string.

                String st = "This is an example string. ";

                        Call Trim instance method.
```

This returns a new string copy. st =

st.Trim(); Console.WriteLine(st);

}

}

Output:

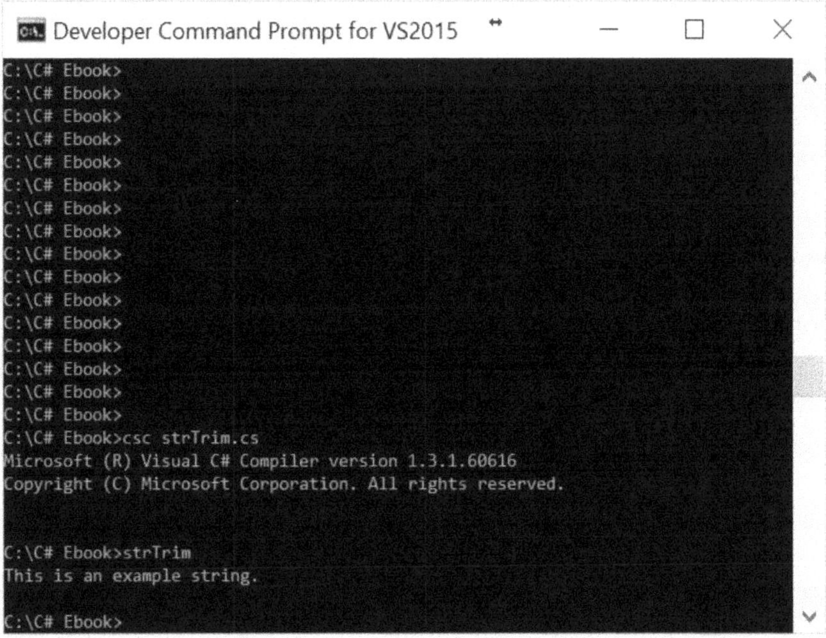
Developer Command Prompt for VS2015
C:\C# Ebook>
C:\C# Ebook>
C:\C# Ebook>
C:\C# Ebook>
C:\C# Ebook>
C:\C# Ebook>
C:\C# Ebook>
C:\C# Ebook>
C:\C# Ebook>
C:\C# Ebook>
C:\C# Ebook>
C:\C# Ebook>
C:\C# Ebook>
C:\C# Ebook>
C:\C# Ebook>
C:\C# Ebook>
C:\C# Ebook>csc strTrim.cs
Microsoft (R) Visual C# Compiler version 1.3.1.60616
Copyright (C) Microsoft Corporation. All rights reserved.
C:\C# Ebook>strTrim
This is an example string.
C:\C# Ebook>

User Input Output

User Input Output is very much similar to any other programming languages I/O. There are Console statements available for these kind of functionalities.

Although you might have already got an idea of the input and output operations by now, a simple C# program will show you how simple it is.

Code:

```
using System;

using System.Collections.Generic; using

 System.Linq;

using System.Text;

 namespace BasicIO

{

        class Program

        {

                static void Main(string[] args)

                {

                        Console.WriteLine("basic I/O Operations");
                //GetData();

                        Console.Write("Enter your coolest name: ");
                string Name

        = Console.ReadLine(); Console.Write("Enter your age: ");
```

```
        string Age = Console.ReadLine();

        //changes echo colour

                //ConsoleColor prevColor =
        Console.ForegroundColor;
                //Console.ForegroundColor = ConsoleColor.red;

        //echo to console

        Console.WriteLine("heya {0}! Your are {1} year(s) old. You
are very young", Name, Age);

        //Restore previous color

        //Console.ForegroundColor = prevColor;

                Console.ReadLine();

                }

        }

}
```

Output:

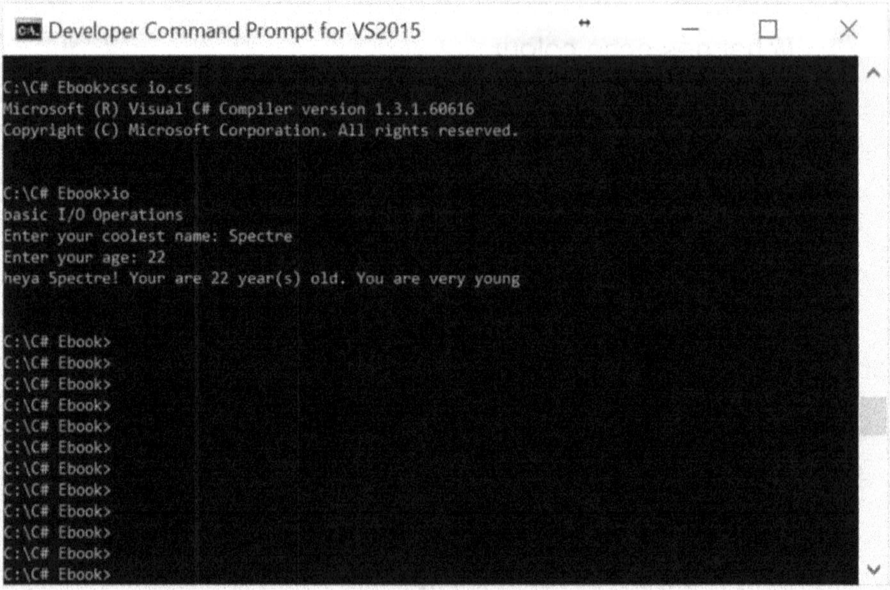
Developer Command Prompt for VS2015
C:\C# Ebook>csc io.cs
Microsoft (R) Visual C# Compiler version 1.3.1.60616
Copyright (C) Microsoft Corporation. All rights reserved.
C:\C# Ebook>io
basic I/O Operations
Enter your coolest name: Spectre
Enter your age: 22
heya Spectre! Your are 22 year(s) old. You are very young
C:\C# Ebook>
C:\C# Ebook>
C:\C# Ebook>
C:\C# Ebook>
C:\C# Ebook>
C:\C# Ebook>
C:\C# Ebook>
C:\C# Ebook>
C:\C# Ebook>
C:\C# Ebook>
C:\C# Ebook>
C:\C# Ebook>

Module - 4 : Control Statements

We have till now studied some of the very basic aspects of programming in C#. Now is the time you really understand what is the use of control statements and conditional statements while developing an efficient code. The flow of a program is altered with the help of these statements which will prove to be of great help while writing code.

Conditional Statements

Mostly, all the control flow statements make use of one or more conditions. To say in layman's terms, when we make a flow statement for a particular action in our program, it first checks the condition, whether it is met and true or false and then proceeds further.

For Example, if we want to compare two values, we use a comparison statement in conditional statement. Thus, if we want to check if one variable is greater than or lesser that the other variable, we use the '>' operator as in x > y . If value of x is greater than the value of y, the statement is true, else the statement is false.

Hereby explained some of the important conditional statements all together:

Equal To (==):

Returns true if the value on the left side of the equation is equal to the value on the right side of the equation.

Example: 3 == 3 is true, while 3 == 4 is false

Not Equal To (!=):

Returns true if the value on the left side of the equation is not equal to the value on the right side of the equation.

Example: 3 != 4 is true, while 3 != 3 is false

Greater Than (>):

Returns true if the value on the left side of the equation is greater than the value on the right side of the equation.

Example: 4 > 3 is true, while 3 > 4 is false

Lesser Than (<):

Returns true if the value on the left side of the equation is lesser than the value on the right side of the equation.

Example: 3 < 4 is true, while 3 < 3 is false

Greater Than or Equal To (>=):

Returns true if the value on the left side of the equation is greater than or equal to the value on the right side of the equation.

Example: 3 >= 3 is true, while 2 >= 3 is false

Lesser Than or Equal To (<=):

Returns true if the value on the left side of the equation is lesser than or equal to the value on the right side of the equation.

Example: 3 <= 4 is true, while 34 <= 3 is false

The AND Operator (&&):

Returns true if all the conditions separated by the && operator are true, else false.

Example: 3 != 4 && 2 == 2 is true, while 3 != 3 && 2 == 2 is false

The OR operator (||):

Returns true if any of the conditions separated by the || OR operator is true, else false.

Example: 3 != 4 || 2 != 2 is true, while 3 != 3 || 4 > 6 is false

The Ternary Operator (?:)

Ternary operator compares two values, and creates a third value that depends on the result of comparison. The ternary operator is very efficient in use and is often used to save the number of lines of code.

A simple program demonstrating the ternary operator is given below:

Code:

```
using System;

class Program
{
    static void Main()
    {

        int value = 100.ToString() == "100" ?
            1 :
            -1;
        Console.WriteLine(value);
```

```
        }
}
```

Output:

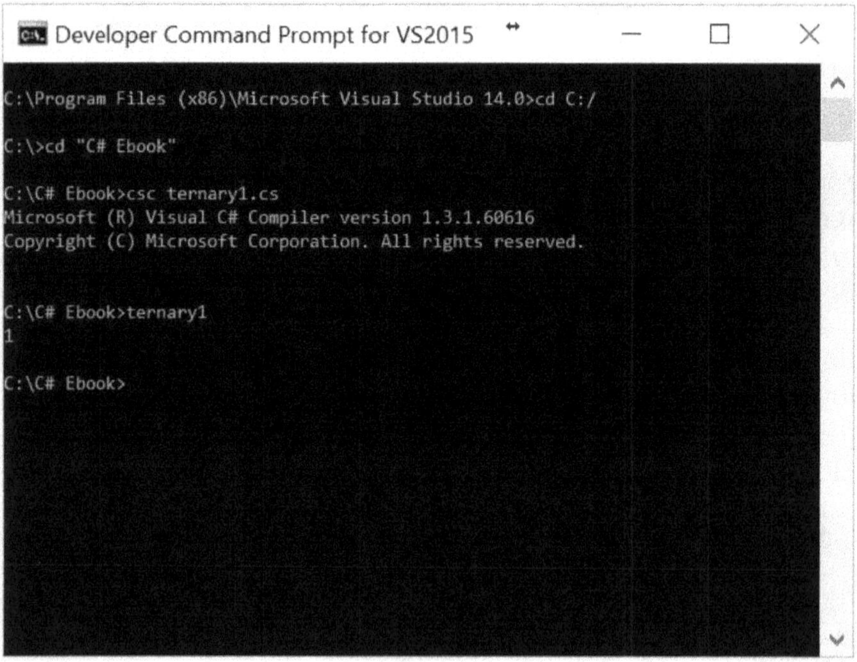
Developer Command Prompt for VS2015
C:\Program Files (x86)\Microsoft Visual Studio 14.0>cd C:/
C:\>cd "C# Ebook"
C:\C# Ebook>csc ternary1.cs
Microsoft (R) Visual C# Compiler version 1.3.1.60616
Copyright (C) Microsoft Corporation. All rights reserved.
C:\C# Ebook>ternary1
1
C:\C# Ebook>

Here are some of the programs mainly using the ternary operator along with other operators that we discussed above.

Returns Ternary Expression

Code:

```
using System;

class Program
```

```
{
        static void Main()
        {
                Console.WriteLine(GetValue("Sam"));
                Console.WriteLine(GetValue("Jane"));
        }

                <summary>

                </summary>
        static int GetValue(string name)
        {
                return name == "Sam" ? 100 : -1;
        }
}
```

Output:

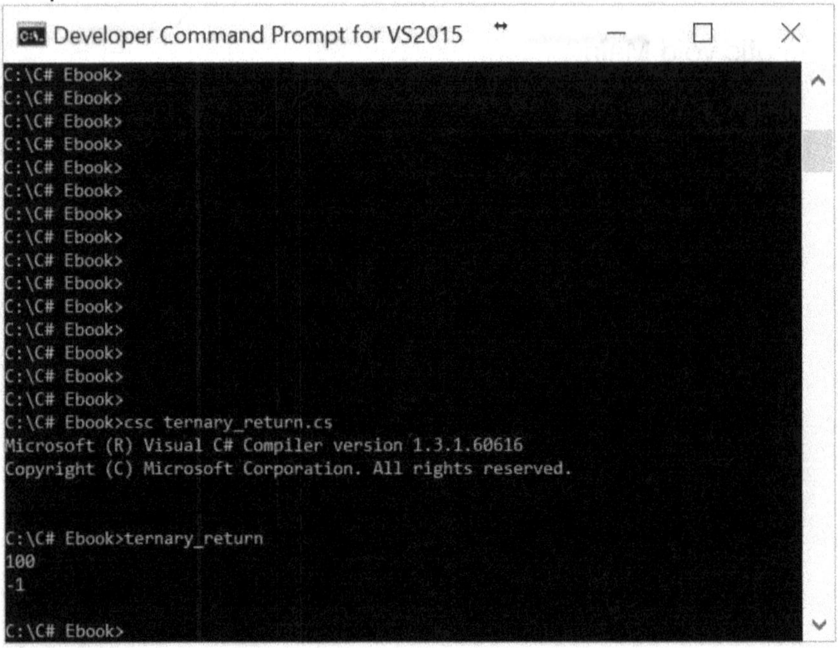
Developer Command Prompt for VS2015
C:\C# Ebook>
C:\C# Ebook>
C:\C# Ebook>
C:\C# Ebook>
C:\C# Ebook>
C:\C# Ebook>
C:\C# Ebook>
C:\C# Ebook>
C:\C# Ebook>
C:\C# Ebook>
C:\C# Ebook>
C:\C# Ebook>
C:\C# Ebook>
C:\C# Ebook>
C:\C# Ebook>
C:\C# Ebook>csc ternary_return.cs
Microsoft (R) Visual C# Compiler version 1.3.1.60616
Copyright (C) Microsoft Corporation. All rights reserved.
C:\C# Ebook>ternary_return
100
-1
C:\C# Ebook>

Implicit Conversion Error

Code:

```
class Program
{
        static void Main()
        {
                int temp = 200;
                int value = temp == 200 ? "bird" : 0;
        }
}
```

Output:

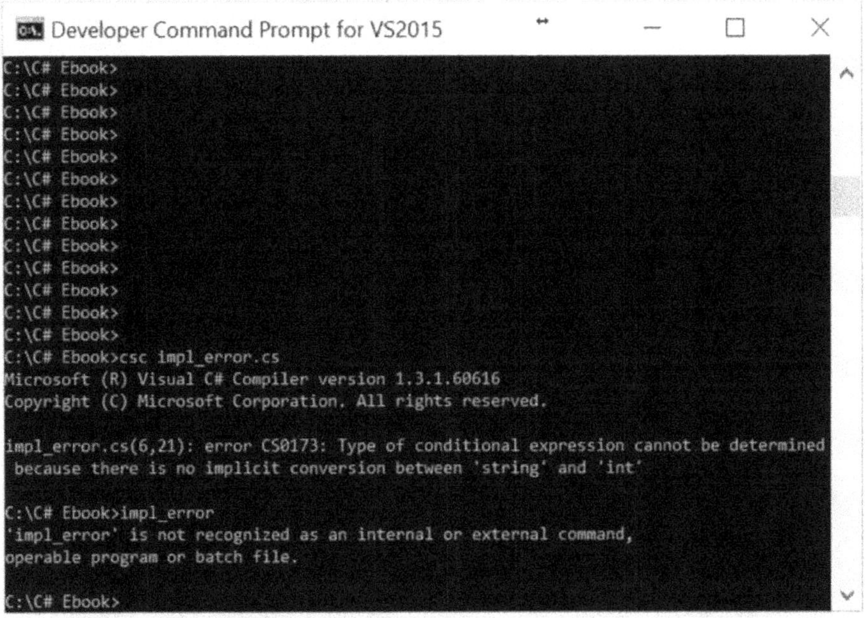
Developer Command Prompt for VS2015
C:\C# Ebook>
C:\C# Ebook>
C:\C# Ebook>
C:\C# Ebook>
C:\C# Ebook>
C:\C# Ebook>
C:\C# Ebook>
C:\C# Ebook>
C:\C# Ebook>
C:\C# Ebook>
C:\C# Ebook>
C:\C# Ebook>
C:\C# Ebook>
C:\C# Ebook>csc impl_error.cs
Microsoft (R) Visual C# Compiler version 1.3.1.60616
Copyright (C) Microsoft Corporation. All rights reserved.
impl_error.cs(6,21): error CS0173: Type of conditional expression cannot be determined because there is no implicit conversion between 'string' and 'int'
C:\C# Ebook>impl_error
'impl_error' is not recognized as an internal or external command,
operable program or batch file.
C:\C# Ebook>

Null Coalescing - If value is null, a value can be specified.

Code:

```
using System;

class Program

{

        static void Main()

        {

                string temp = null;

                string value1 = temp ?? "bird";
        Console.WriteLine("NULL
                COALESCING: " + value1); // Use ternary for same
```

```
result.
        string value2 = temp == null ? "bird" : temp;
        Console.WriteLine("TERNARY: " + value2);
    }
}
```

Output:

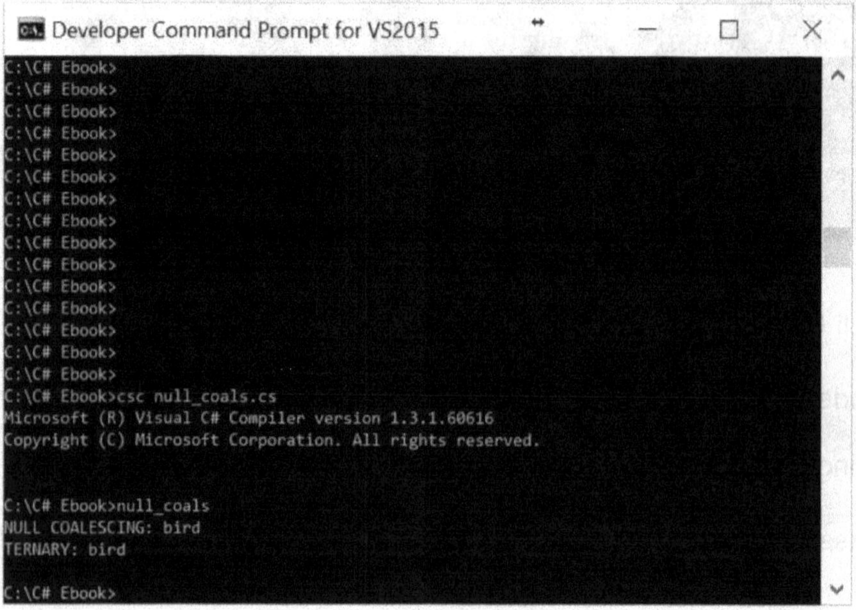
Developer Command Prompt for VS2015
C:\C# Ebook>
C:\C# Ebook>
C:\C# Ebook>
C:\C# Ebook>
C:\C# Ebook>
C:\C# Ebook>
C:\C# Ebook>
C:\C# Ebook>
C:\C# Ebook>
C:\C# Ebook>
C:\C# Ebook>
C:\C# Ebook>
C:\C# Ebook>
C:\C# Ebook>
C:\C# Ebook>
C:\C# Ebook>csc null_coals.cs
Microsoft (R) Visual C# Compiler version 1.3.1.60616
Copyright (C) Microsoft Corporation. All rights reserved.
C:\C# Ebook>null_coals
NULL COALESCING: bird
TERNARY: bird
C:\C# Ebook>

Control Flow Statements

We have now mastered the art of using the condition statements. Let's have a look at how to use these statements in controlling the flow of program via control flow statements.

A loop statement is used to repeatedly execute a statement or a group of statements. We now discuss various loop statements in detail now:

If Statement:

If statement is used to detect if a condition is true. A simple program will explain this in a very good manner.

Code:

```
using System;


class Program

{

        static void Main()

        {

                int value = 10 / 2; if

                 (value == 5)

                {

                        Console.WriteLine(true);

                }

        }

}
```

Output:

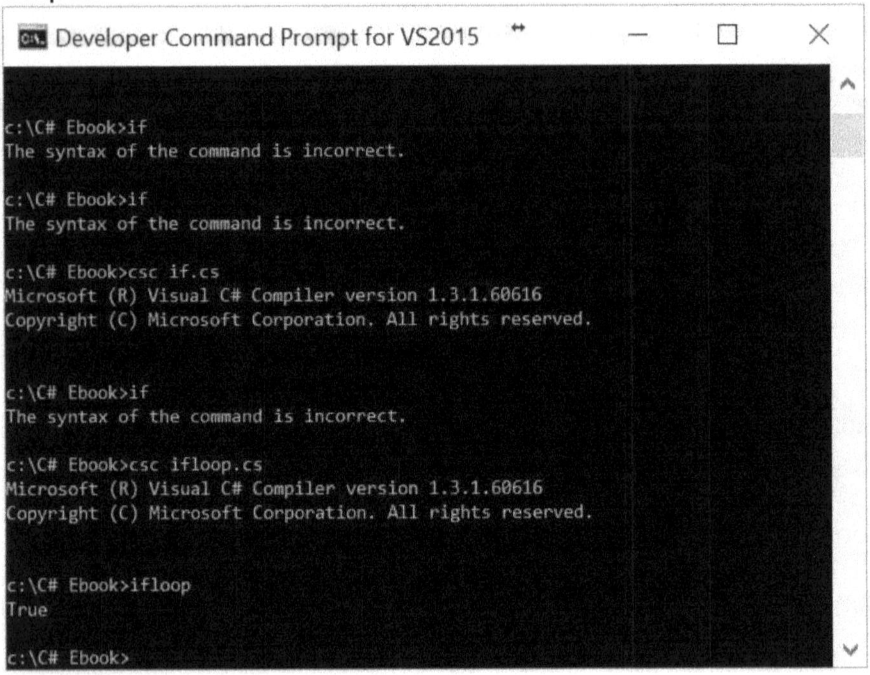
Developer Command Prompt for VS2015
c:\C# Ebook>if
The syntax of the command is incorrect.
c:\C# Ebook>if
The syntax of the command is incorrect.
c:\C# Ebook>csc if.cs
Microsoft (R) Visual C# Compiler version 1.3.1.60616
Copyright (C) Microsoft Corporation. All rights reserved.
c:\C# Ebook>if
The syntax of the command is incorrect.
c:\C# Ebook>csc ifloop.cs
Microsoft (R) Visual C# Compiler version 1.3.1.60616
Copyright (C) Microsoft Corporation. All rights reserved.
c:\C# Ebook>ifloop
True
c:\C# Ebook>

Else if and Else Statement

With the if statement, we check a condition and go on, but what if we want to check another condition after a preliminary condition. We use Else-if statement at this point. Finally, we use an else statement to specify what to do in case any of the if or the else if statements don't turn up to be true.

A simple program will clear the understanding issues faced:

Code:

```
using System;

class Program

{
```

```
static void Main()
{
        embedded if-statement three times. int result1
        = Test(0);
      int result2 = Test(50); int
       result3 = Test(-1);
            Print results.
        Console.WriteLine(result1);
        Console.WriteLine(result2);
      Console.WriteLine(result3);
}
static int Test(int value)
{
      if (value == 0)
      {
            return -1;
      }
      else if (value <= 10)
      {
            return 0;
      }
```

```
            else if (value <= 100)
            {
                  return 1;
            }
            else
            {
                  return 2;
            }
      }
}
```

Output:

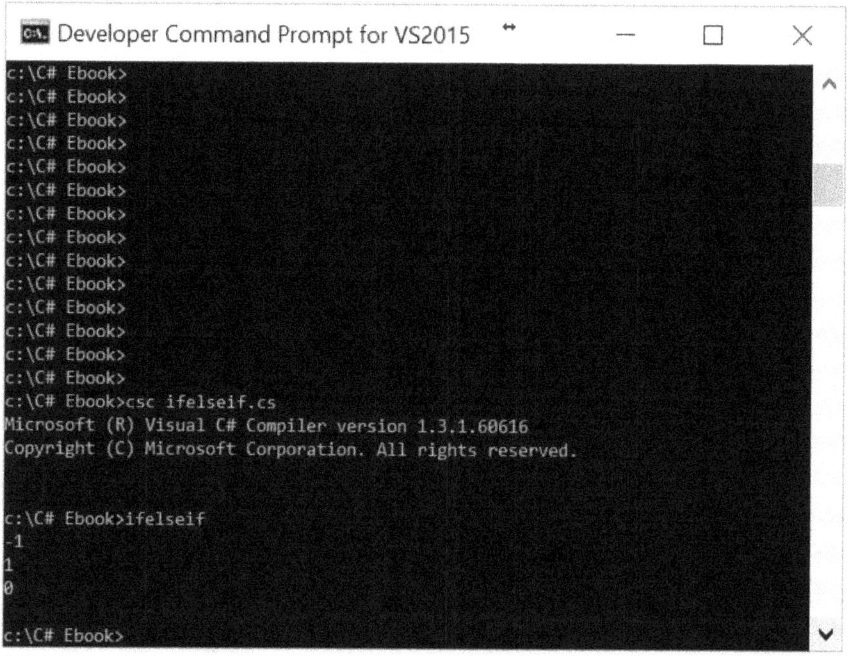
Developer Command Prompt for VS2015
c:\C# Ebook>
c:\C# Ebook>
c:\C# Ebook>
c:\C# Ebook>
c:\C# Ebook>
c:\C# Ebook>
c:\C# Ebook>
c:\C# Ebook>
c:\C# Ebook>
c:\C# Ebook>
c:\C# Ebook>
c:\C# Ebook>
c:\C# Ebook>
c:\C# Ebook>
c:\C# Ebook>csc ifelseif.cs
Microsoft (R) Visual C# Compiler version 1.3.1.60616
Copyright (C) Microsoft Corporation. All rights reserved.
c:\C# Ebook>ifelseif
-1
1
0
c:\C# Ebook>

Else block is used to maintain symmetry. A program that shows simple else constructs will be useful:

Code:

```
using System;

class Program

{

    static void Main()

    {

        Console.WriteLine(A(5));

        Console.WriteLine(B(4));

    }
```

```
        static bool A(int y)
        {
            if (y >= 5)
            {
                return true;
            }
            else
            {
                return false;
            }
        }

        static bool B(int y)
        {
            if (y >= 5)
            {
                return true;
            }
            return false;
        }
}
```

Output:

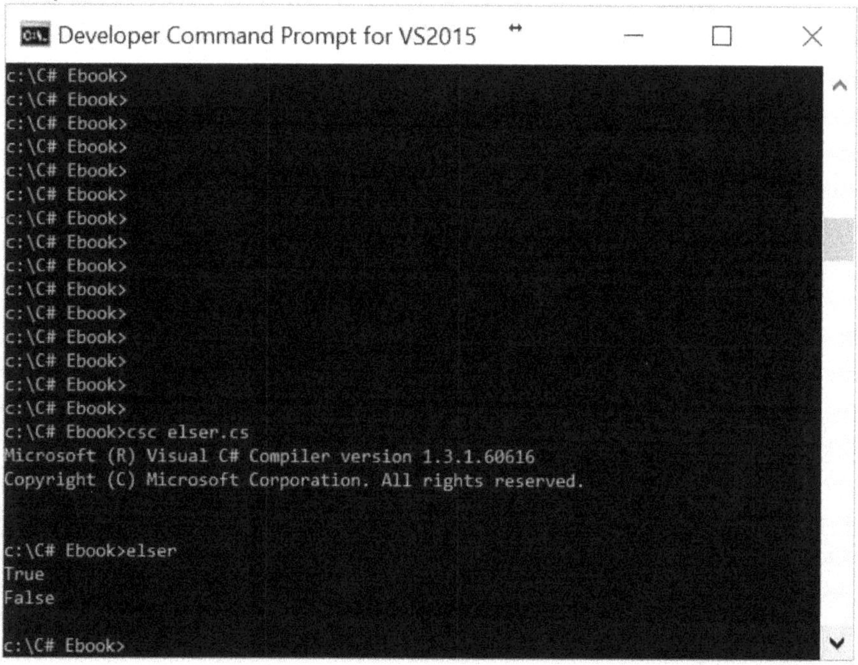
Developer Command Prompt for VS2015
c:\C# Ebook>
c:\C# Ebook>
c:\C# Ebook>
c:\C# Ebook>
c:\C# Ebook>
c:\C# Ebook>
c:\C# Ebook>
c:\C# Ebook>
c:\C# Ebook>
c:\C# Ebook>
c:\C# Ebook>
c:\C# Ebook>
c:\C# Ebook>
c:\C# Ebook>
c:\C# Ebook>
c:\C# Ebook>csc elser.cs
Microsoft (R) Visual C# Compiler version 1.3.1.60616
Copyright (C) Microsoft Corporation. All rights reserved.
c:\C# Ebook>elser
True
False
c:\C# Ebook>

Now we see some programs which will highlight the use of conditional statements as well as the loops.

A program that uses if and expressions:

Code:

```
using System;

class Program

{

        static void Main()

        {

                int a = 1; int

                b = 3;
```

```
            // Use negated expression. if (!(a
             == 1 && b == 2))
            {
                Console.WriteLine(true);
            }

            // Use binary or version. if (a != 1 ||
             b != 2)
            {
                Console.WriteLine(true);
            }
        }
}
```

Output:

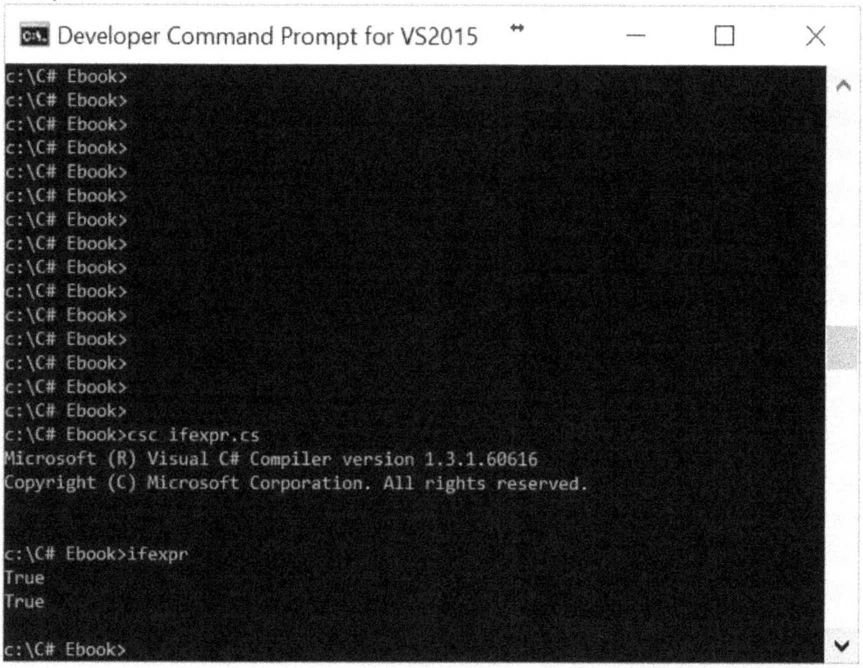
Developer Command Prompt for VS2015
c:\C# Ebook>
c:\C# Ebook>
c:\C# Ebook>
c:\C# Ebook>
c:\C# Ebook>
c:\C# Ebook>
c:\C# Ebook>
c:\C# Ebook>
c:\C# Ebook>
c:\C# Ebook>
c:\C# Ebook>
c:\C# Ebook>
c:\C# Ebook>
c:\C# Ebook>
c:\C# Ebook>
c:\C# Ebook>csc ifexpr.cs
Microsoft (R) Visual C# Compiler version 1.3.1.60616
Copyright (C) Microsoft Corporation. All rights reserved.
c:\C# Ebook>ifexpr
True
True
c:\C# Ebook>

A program that doesn’t use brackets:

Code:

```
using System;

class Program

{

        static void Main()

        {

                int value = 1; int

                 size = 2;
```

```
            if (value == 1) if (size ==

                2)

                Console.WriteLine("1, 2");


            if (value == 0)

                Console.WriteLine("0"); // Not reached.

            else

                Console.WriteLine("Not 0"); // Reached.


            if (value == 2) Console.WriteLine("2"); // Not
        reached.

        }

}
```

Output:

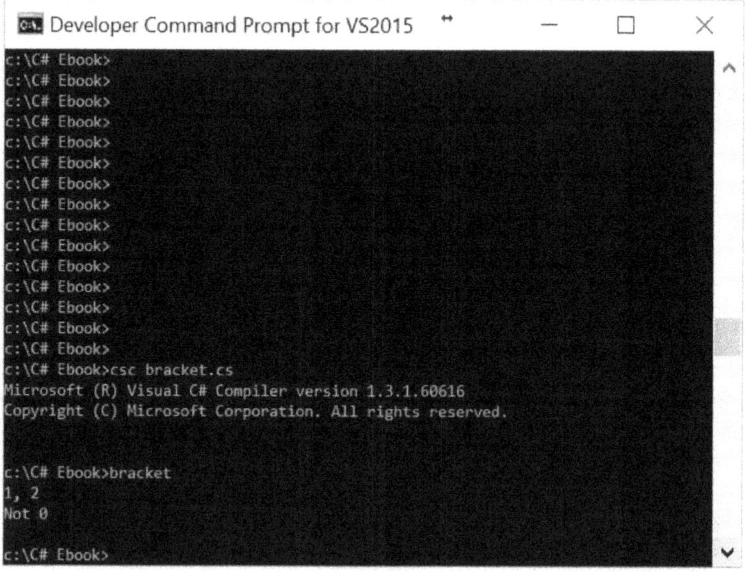
Developer Command Prompt for VS2015
c:\C# Ebook>
c:\C# Ebook>
c:\C# Ebook>
c:\C# Ebook>
c:\C# Ebook>
c:\C# Ebook>
c:\C# Ebook>
c:\C# Ebook>
c:\C# Ebook>
c:\C# Ebook>
c:\C# Ebook>
c:\C# Ebook>
c:\C# Ebook>
c:\C# Ebook>
c:\C# Ebook>
c:\C# Ebook>csc bracket.cs
Microsoft (R) Visual C# Compiler version 1.3.1.60616
Copyright (C) Microsoft Corporation. All rights reserved.
c:\C# Ebook>bracket
1, 2
Not 0
c:\C# Ebook>

A nested if program example:

Code:

```
using System;

class Program

{

    static void Main()

    {

        Method1(50);

        Method2(50);

        Method3(50);

    }

    static void Method1(int value)
```

```
{
    if (value >= 10)
    {
        if (value <= 100)
        {
            Console.WriteLine(true);
        }
    }
}
static void Method2(int value)
{
    if (value >= 10 && value <= 100)
    {
        Console.WriteLine(true);
    }
}
static void Method3(int value)
{
    if (value <= 100 && value
        >= 10)
    {
```

```
                    Console.WriteLine(true);
            }
        }
}
```

Output:

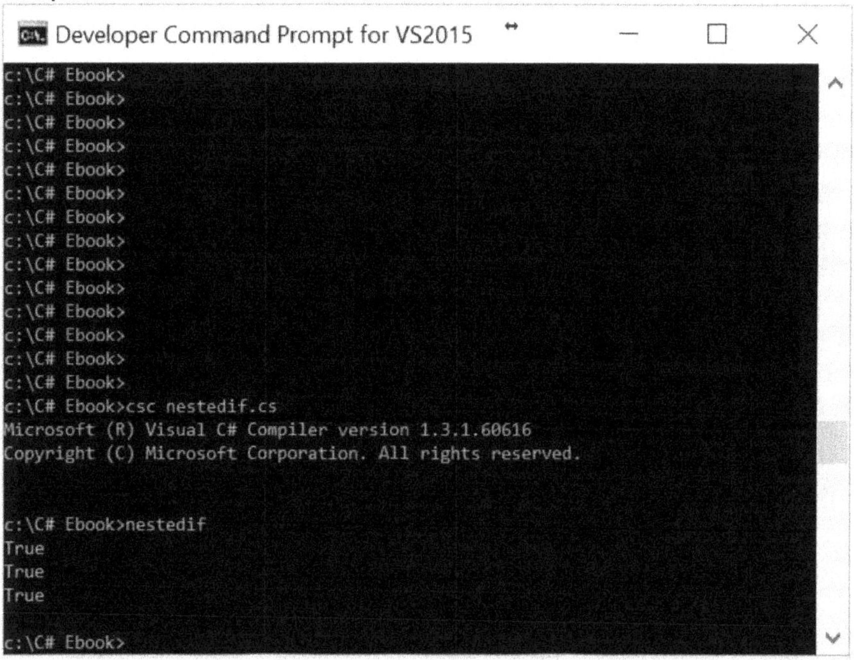
Developer Command Prompt for VS2015
c:\C# Ebook>
c:\C# Ebook>
c:\C# Ebook>
c:\C# Ebook>
c:\C# Ebook>
c:\C# Ebook>
c:\C# Ebook>
c:\C# Ebook>
c:\C# Ebook>
c:\C# Ebook>
c:\C# Ebook>
c:\C# Ebook>
c:\C# Ebook>
c:\C# Ebook>
c:\C# Ebook>csc nestedif.cs
Microsoft (R) Visual C# Compiler version 1.3.1.60616
Copyright (C) Microsoft Corporation. All rights reserved.
c:\C# Ebook>nestedif
True
True
True
c:\C# Ebook>

A variable cannot be assigned in a c# program if statement. It will simply throw out an compilation error as shown here:

Code:

```
class Program
{
        static void Main()
        {
                int i = 100;
```

```
                // This does not compile!
                if (i = 200)
                {
                        System.Console.WriteLine("Zebra");
                }
        }
}
```

Output:

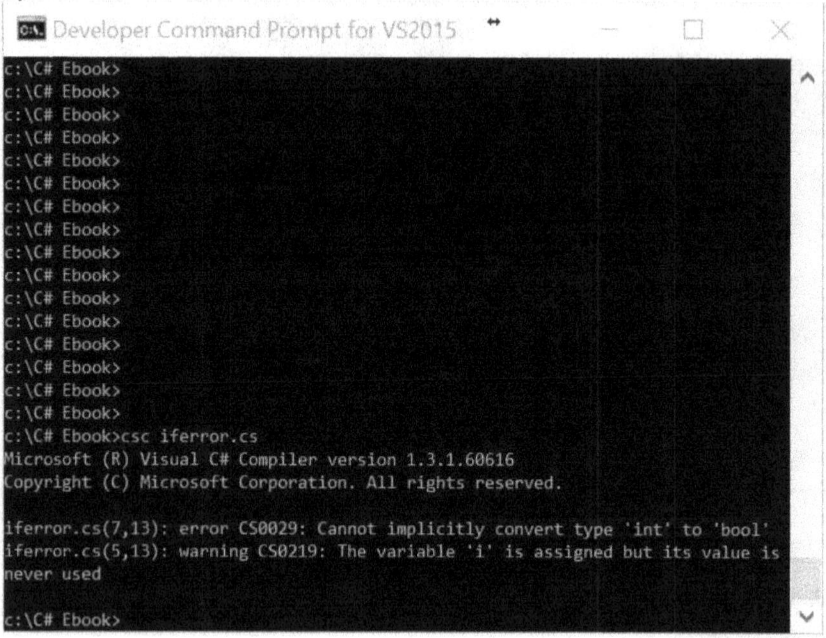
Developer Command Prompt for VS2015
c:\C# Ebook>
c:\C# Ebook>
c:\C# Ebook>
c:\C# Ebook>
c:\C# Ebook>
c:\C# Ebook>
c:\C# Ebook>
c:\C# Ebook>
c:\C# Ebook>
c:\C# Ebook>
c:\C# Ebook>
c:\C# Ebook>
c:\C# Ebook>
c:\C# Ebook>
c:\C# Ebook>
c:\C# Ebook>
c:\C# Ebook>csc iferror.cs
Microsoft (R) Visual C# Compiler version 1.3.1.60616
Copyright (C) Microsoft Corporation. All rights reserved.
iferror.cs(7,13): error CS0029: Cannot implicitly convert type 'int' to 'bool'
iferror.cs(5,13): warning CS0219: The variable 'i' is assigned but its value is never used
c:\C# Ebook>

We get a specific error like this: “Cannot implicitly convert type ‘int’ to ‘bool’ ”

Switch Statement:

A switch statement is used when a variable is checked for a condition against a list of values. It is very easy to use and convenient.

We will now see a program explaining the switch statement's effects:

Code:

```
using System;

class Program

{

        static void Main()

        {

                int value = 5;

                 switch (value)

                {

                        case 1: Console.WriteLine(1);

                                break;

                        case 5: Console.WriteLine(5);

                                break;

                }

        }

}
```

Output:

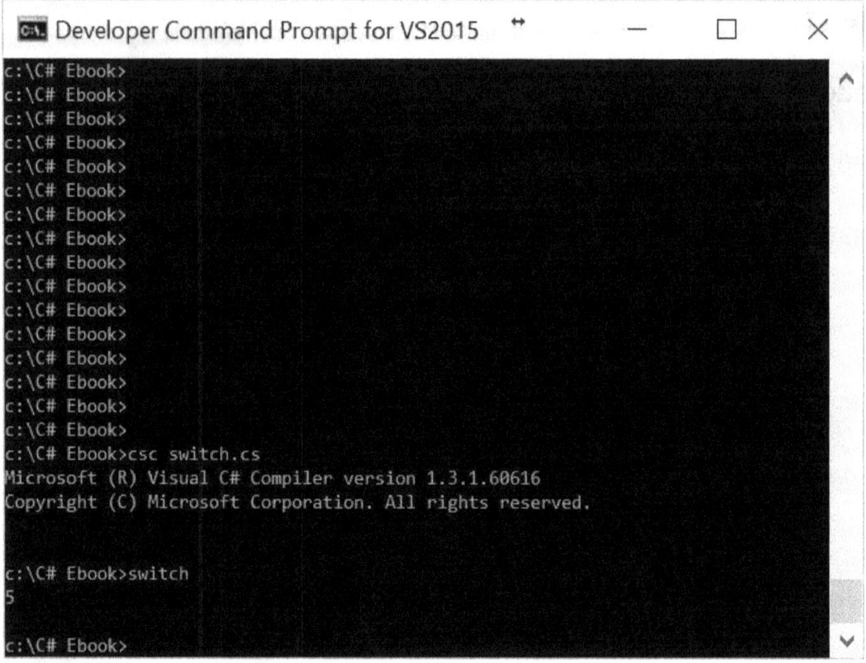
Developer Command Prompt for VS2015
c:\C# Ebook>
c:\C# Ebook>
c:\C# Ebook>
c:\C# Ebook>
c:\C# Ebook>
c:\C# Ebook>
c:\C# Ebook>
c:\C# Ebook>
c:\C# Ebook>
c:\C# Ebook>
c:\C# Ebook>
c:\C# Ebook>
c:\C# Ebook>
c:\C# Ebook>
c:\C# Ebook>
c:\C# Ebook>
c:\C# Ebook>csc switch.cs
Microsoft (R) Visual C# Compiler version 1.3.1.60616
Copyright (C) Microsoft Corporation. All rights reserved.
c:\C# Ebook>switch
5
c:\C# Ebook>

Now we see different types of variations one can do while using the switch statement Program using int switch:

Code:

```
class Program

{

        static void Main()

        {

                while (true)

                {

                        System.Console.WriteLine("Type number
                and press Return");
```

```
try
{
    Int I =
int.Parse(System.Console.ReadLine()); switch(i)
    {
        case 0:
        case 1:
        case 2:
            {
                System.Console.
            WriteLine("Low
            number");
                break;
            }
        case 3:
        case 4:
        case 5:
            {
                System.Console.
            WriteLine("Medium
            number");
                break;
            }
```

```
                    default:
                        {
                            System.Console.WriteLine("Other number");
                            break;
                        }
                }
            }
            catch
            {
            }
        }
    }
}
```

Output:

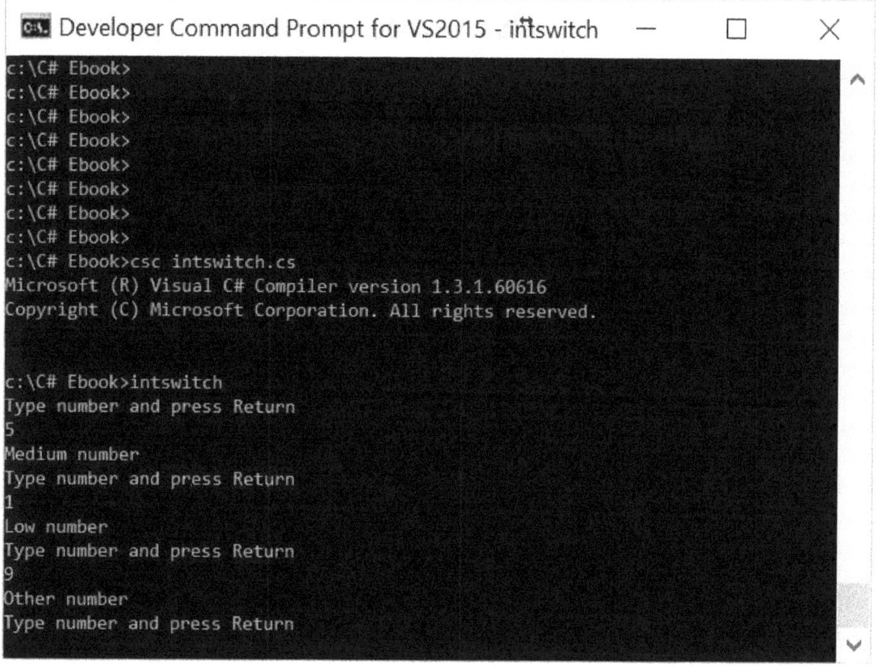
Developer Command Prompt for VS2015 - intswitch
c:\C# Ebook>
c:\C# Ebook>
c:\C# Ebook>
c:\C# Ebook>
c:\C# Ebook>
c:\C# Ebook>
c:\C# Ebook>
c:\C# Ebook>
c:\C# Ebook>csc intswitch.cs
Microsoft (R) Visual C# Compiler version 1.3.1.60616
Copyright (C) Microsoft Corporation. All rights reserved.
c:\C# Ebook>intswitch
Type number and press Return
5
Medium number
Type number and press Return
1
Low number
Type number and press Return
9
Other number
Type number and press Return

Program using string switch:

Code:

```
using System;
class Program
{
    static void Main()
    {
        string value = "turnip";
        // ... Switch on the string. Switch
        (value)
        {
```

```
                    case "lettuce":
                        Console.WriteLine("LETTUCE");
                        break;
                    case "squash":
                        Console.WriteLine("SQUASH");
                        break;
                    case "turnip":
                        Console.WriteLine("TURNIP");
                        break;
               }
          }
}
```

Output:

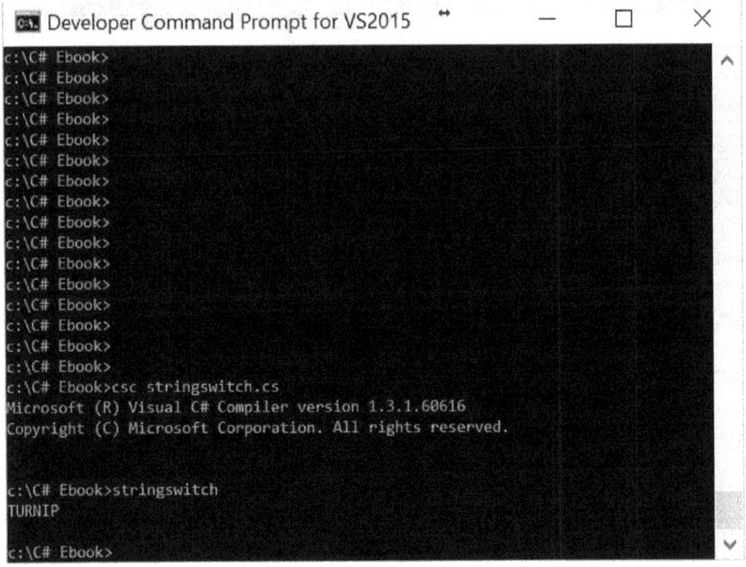
Developer Command Prompt for VS2015
c:\C# Ebook>
c:\C# Ebook>
c:\C# Ebook>
c:\C# Ebook>
c:\C# Ebook>
c:\C# Ebook>
c:\C# Ebook>
c:\C# Ebook>
c:\C# Ebook>
c:\C# Ebook>
c:\C# Ebook>
c:\C# Ebook>
c:\C# Ebook>
c:\C# Ebook>
c:\C# Ebook>
c:\C# Ebook>
c:\C# Ebook>csc stringswitch.cs
Microsoft (R) Visual C# Compiler version 1.3.1.60616
Copyright (C) Microsoft Corporation. All rights reserved.
c:\C# Ebook>stringswitch
TURNIP
c:\C# Ebook>

Program using nested switch:

Code:

```
using System;

class Program

{

        static void Main()

        {

                int[] array = { 4, 10, 14 }; switch

                (array[0])

                {

                        case 3:

                                Console.WriteLine(3); // Not reached.
                        break;

                        case 4: Console.WriteLine(4);

                                // ... Use nested switch. switch

                                (array[1])

                                {

                                        case 10:
                                Console.WriteLine(10);

                                                break;

                                }
```

```
break;

}

}

}
```

Output:

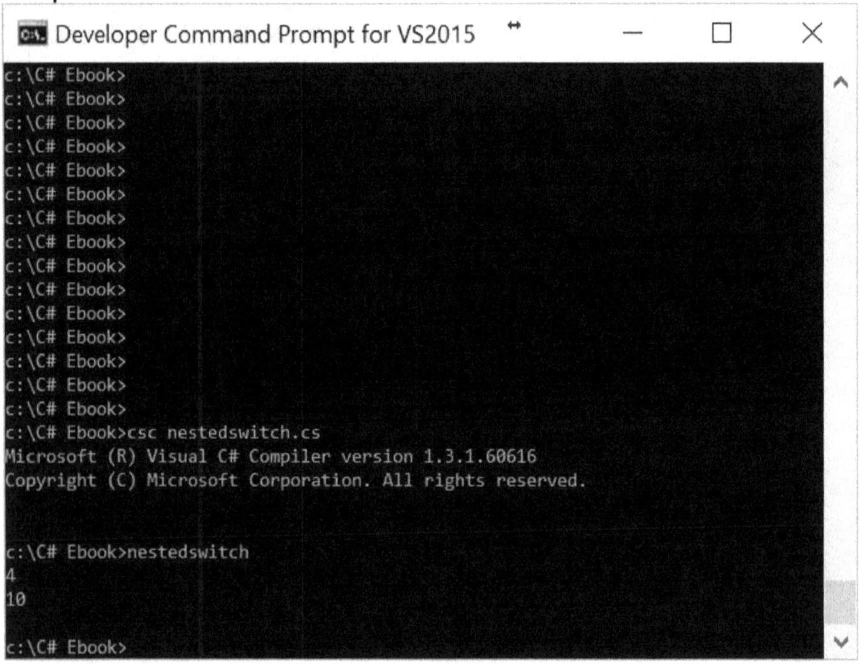
Developer Command Prompt for VS2015
c:\C# Ebook>
c:\C# Ebook>
c:\C# Ebook>
c:\C# Ebook>
c:\C# Ebook>
c:\C# Ebook>
c:\C# Ebook>
c:\C# Ebook>
c:\C# Ebook>
c:\C# Ebook>
c:\C# Ebook>
c:\C# Ebook>
c:\C# Ebook>
c:\C# Ebook>
c:\C# Ebook>
c:\C# Ebook>csc nestedswitch.cs
Microsoft (R) Visual C# Compiler version 1.3.1.60616
Copyright (C) Microsoft Corporation. All rights reserved.
c:\C# Ebook>nestedswitch
4
10
c:\C# Ebook>

A C# program that benchmarks switch statements. It can prove to be very efficient while calculating microseconds:

Code:

```
using System;

using System.Diagnostics;

class Program

{
```

```
static int Method1(int v)
{
        switch (v)
        {
                case 0:
                        return 10;
                case 1:
                        return -1;
                case 2:
                        return 20;
                default:
                        return 0;
        }
}
static int Method2(int v)
{
        if (v == 0) return 10; if (v ==
        1)  return -1; if (v == 2) return
        20; return 0;
}
```

```
static void Main()
{
        Method1(0); Method2(0); const int
        max = 100000000;
        var s1 = Stopwatch.StartNew(); for (int i
        = 0; i < max; i++)
        {
                Method1(0);
                Method1(1);
                Method1(2);
                Method1(3);
        }
        s1.Stop();
        var s2 = Stopwatch.StartNew(); for (int i
        = 0; i < max; i++)
        {
                Method2(0);
                Method2(1);
                Method2(2);
                Method2(3);
        }
```

```
            s2.Stop();

            Console.WriteLine(((double)(s1.Elapsed.TotalMillis
        econds * 1000000) /

                max).ToString("0.00 ns"));

            Console.WriteLine(((double)(s2.Elapsed.TotalMillis
        econds * 1000000) /

                max).ToString("0.00 ns"));

            Console.Read();

        }

}
```

Output:

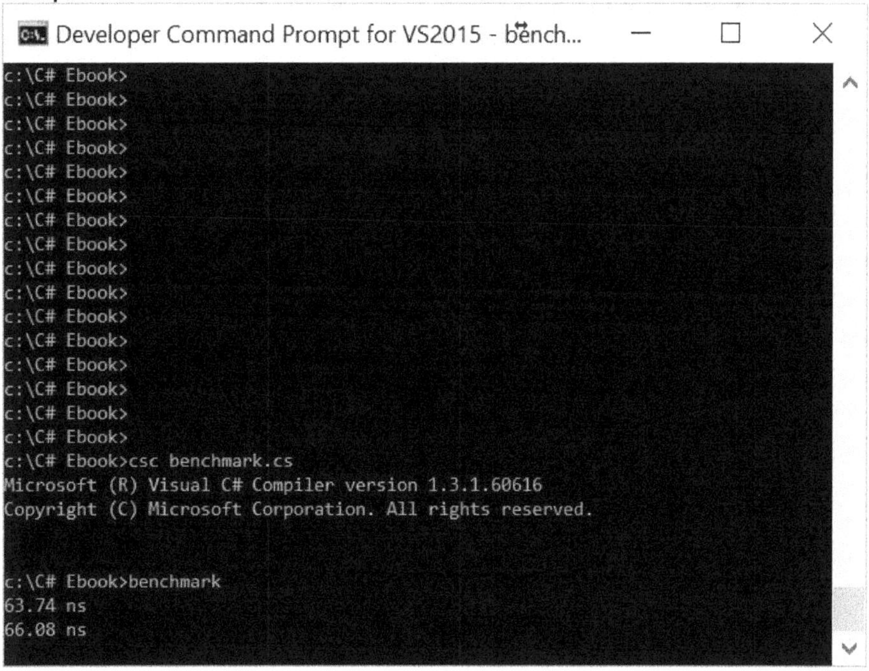
Developer Command Prompt for VS2015 - bench...
c:\C# Ebook>
c:\C# Ebook>
c:\C# Ebook>
c:\C# Ebook>
c:\C# Ebook>
c:\C# Ebook>
c:\C# Ebook>
c:\C# Ebook>
c:\C# Ebook>
c:\C# Ebook>
c:\C# Ebook>
c:\C# Ebook>
c:\C# Ebook>
c:\C# Ebook>
c:\C# Ebook>
c:\C# Ebook>
c:\C# Ebook>csc benchmark.cs
Microsoft (R) Visual C# Compiler version 1.3.1.60616
Copyright (C) Microsoft Corporation. All rights reserved.
c:\C# Ebook>benchmark
63.74 ns
66.08 ns

Type matching using switch statements:

Code:

```
using System;

class Animal
{
        public int size;
}

class Bird : Animal
{
        public int color;
}

class Cat : Animal
{
        public bool wild;
}
class Program
{
        static void Test(Animal animal)
        {
                // Switch on a class type with pattern matching.
```

```
switch (animal)

    {

        case Cat c:

            Console.WriteLine($"CAT wild =
        {c.wild}"); break;

        case Bird b:

            Console.WriteLine($"BIRD color =
        {b.color}"); break;

        case Animal a:

            Console.WriteLine($"ANIMAL size =
        {a.size}"); break;

    }

}

static void Main()

{

    // Create some class instances. Cat cat =

    new Cat();

    cat.wild = true;

    Bird bird = new Bird();

    bird.color = 5;

    Animal animal = new Animal();

    animal.size = 10;
```

```
            // Test class instances.

            Test(cat);

            Test(bird);

            Test(animal);

        }

}
```

Output:

CAT wild = True

BIRD color = 5

ANIMAL size = 10

Pattern Matching with switch statement:

Code:

```
using System; using System;
class Program
{
    static void Main()
    {
        int value = 200;
        int secondValue = 300;
        // Use switch with pattern matching. switch
        (value)
        {
            case 200 when secondValue == 0:
            Console.WriteLine("Y"); break;
            case 200 when secondValue == 300:
        Console.WriteLine("Value is 200, secondValue is
        300");
```

```
                break;
            case 400:
                Console.WriteLine("Z");
                break;
        }
    }
}
```

Output:

Value is 200, secondValue is 300

For Loops:

Multiple execution of a sequence of statements is done by for loops, and also management of loop variable is done by this. Generally the variable 'i' is used as a standard convention for other programmers to understand.

There are three main parts of the for loop:

- Start
- End

3. Increment

Start: The first element always starts from the 0 element or value.

End: The loop ends when the preset condition is met for the variable i.

Increment: The increment is done after each iteration in the for loop

A basic C# for loop is given below:

Code:

```
using System;

class Program
{
    static void Main()
    {
        for (int i = 0; i < 10; i++)
        {
            Console.WriteLine(i);
        }
    }
}
```

Output:

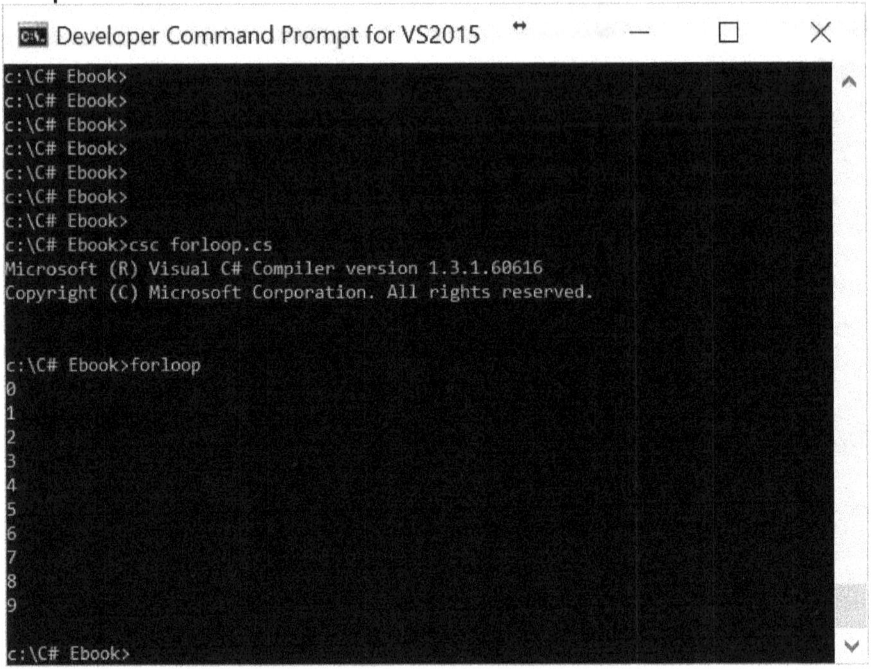
Developer Command Prompt for VS2015
c:\C# Ebook>
c:\C# Ebook>
c:\C# Ebook>
c:\C# Ebook>
c:\C# Ebook>
c:\C# Ebook>
c:\C# Ebook>
c:\C# Ebook>csc forloop.cs
Microsoft (R) Visual C# Compiler version 1.3.1.60616
Copyright (C) Microsoft Corporation. All rights reserved.
c:\C# Ebook>forloop
0
1
2
3
4
5
6
7
8
9
c:\C# Ebook>

The same works for decrement too. Example:

Code:

```
using System;

class Program

{

        static void Main()

        {

                for (int i = 10 - 1; i >= 0; i--)

                {

                        Console.WriteLine(i);
```

```
        }
    }
}
```

Output:

9

8

7

6

5

4

3

2

1

0

Step Incremental For Loop. Example:

Code:

```
using System;
class Program
{
    static void Main()
    {
```

```
            for (int i = 0; i < 10; i += 3)
            {
                Console.WriteLine(i);
            }
        }
}
```

Output:

```
0
3
6
9
12
```

Step Decremental For Loop. Example:

Code:

```
using System;
class Program
{
        static void Main()
        {
            for (int i = 10 - 1; i >= 0; i -= 2)
```

```
        {
            Console.WriteLine(i);
        }
    }
}
```

Output:

9

7

5

3

1

Expression in Maximum boundaries For Loop. Example:

Code:

```
using System;
class Program
{
    static void Main()
    {
        for (int i = 0; i < (20 / 2); i += 2)
        {
            Console.WriteLine(i);
```

```
        }
    }
}
```

Output:

0

2

4

6

8

Character ranges can also be defined in For Loop. Example :

Code:

```
using System;
class Program
{
    static void Main()
    {
        // ... Loop over character range. for (char c =
        'a'; c <= 'z'; c++)
        {
            Console.WriteLine(c);
        }
    }
```

}
Output:

```
a b
c d
e....
```

Foreach loop:

In foreach loop, evaluation of each element is done separately. No need for any index variable and this makes writing programs with each loop fairly simple and easy. You have seen for each loop previously in this book and you might have got the pattern, but if not, I am stating some examples for you to understand and develop the pattern.

A simple foreach over array:

Code:

```
using System;

class Program

{

        static void Main()

        {

                string[] pets = { "dog", "cat", "bird" };
                // ... Loop with the foreach keyword. foreach (string
        value in pets)
                {

                        Console.WriteLine(value);

                }
```

```
        }
}
```

Output:

```
dog
cat
Bird
```

A foreach LINQ :

Code:

```
using System; using
System.Linq;

class Program

{

        static void Main()

        {

                // An unsorted string array.

                string[] letters = { "d", "c", "a", "b" }; // Use LINQ
                query syntax to sort the array alphabetically.

                var sorted = from letter in letters orderby letter

                                select letter;

                // Loop with the foreach keyword. foreach
                (string value in sorted)
                {

                        Console.WriteLine(value);

                }
```

```
        }
}
```

Output:

```
a
b
c
d
```

A basic C# foreach loop which uses list and remove is given below:

Code:

```
using System;

using System.Collections.Generic;

class Program

{

        static void Main()

        {

                List<int> list = new List<int>(); list.Add(1);

                list.Add(2);

                list.Add(3);

                        Loop over list elements using foreach-loop.
                foreach (int element in list)

                {

                        Console.WriteLine(element);
```

```
        }
```

You can't remove elements in a foreach-loop.

```
        try
        {
            foreach (int element in list)
            {
                list.Remove(element);
            }
        }
        catch (Exception ex)
        {
            Console.WriteLine(ex.Message);
        }
    }
}
```

Output:

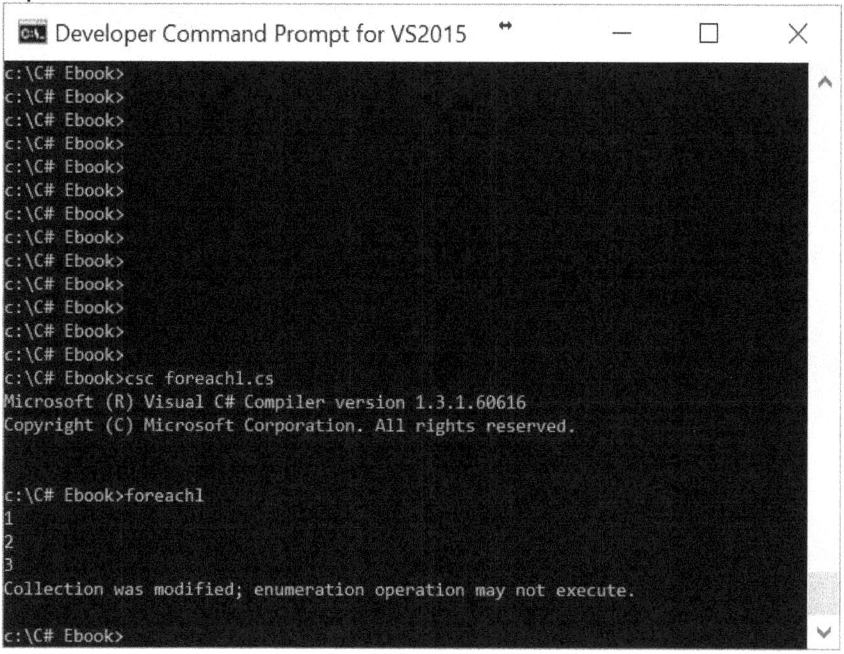
Developer Command Prompt for VS2015
c:\C# Ebook>
c:\C# Ebook>
c:\C# Ebook>
c:\C# Ebook>
c:\C# Ebook>
c:\C# Ebook>
c:\C# Ebook>
c:\C# Ebook>
c:\C# Ebook>
c:\C# Ebook>
c:\C# Ebook>
c:\C# Ebook>
c:\C# Ebook>
c:\C# Ebook>csc foreach1.cs
Microsoft (R) Visual C# Compiler version 1.3.1.60616
Copyright (C) Microsoft Corporation. All rights reserved.
c:\C# Ebook>foreach1
1
2
3
Collection was modified; enumeration operation may not execute.
c:\C# Ebook>

For and foreach loops program:

Code:

```
using System;

class Program
{
        static void Main()
        {
                // Array of color strings.
                        string[] colors = { "red", "orange", "yellow",
                "green" };

                // Print all colors with for-loop.
                Console.WriteLine(":::FOR:::");
                for (int i = 0; i < colors.Length; i++)
                {
                        // Assign string reference based on induction
variable.
                        string value = colors[i];
                        Console.WriteLine(value);
                }

                // Print all colors with for each.
```

```
            Console.WriteLine(":::FOREACH:::"); foreach
            (var value in colors)
            {
                Console.WriteLine(value);
            }
        }
}
```

Output:

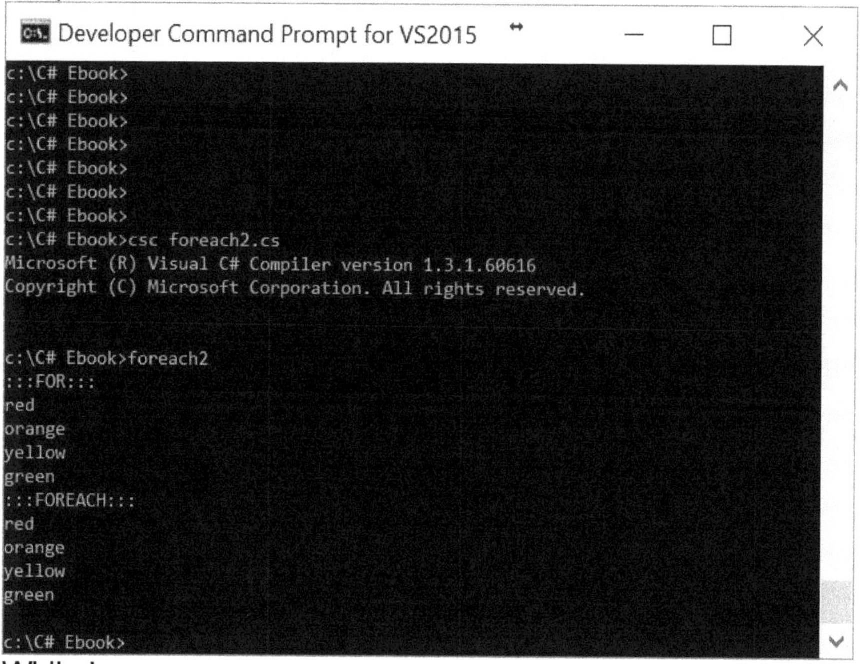
Developer Command Prompt for VS2015
c:\C# Ebook>
c:\C# Ebook>
c:\C# Ebook>
c:\C# Ebook>
c:\C# Ebook>
c:\C# Ebook>
c:\C# Ebook>
c:\C# Ebook>csc foreach2.cs
Microsoft (R) Visual C# Compiler version 1.3.1.60616
Copyright (C) Microsoft Corporation. All rights reserved.
c:\C# Ebook>foreach2
:::FOR:::
red
orange
yellow
green
:::FOREACH:::
red
orange
yellow
green
c:\C# Ebook>

While Loop

A while loop is ever going until the expression is false. Some loops are not good for just a simple range of numbers, while loops works best here. Here, the expression is calculated each time and if the result is true, the loop's body statements are executed.

Some programs to better understand the working of the while loop:

Code:

```
using System;

class Program

{

        static void Main()

        {

                int i = 0;

                while (i < 10)

                {

                        Console.Write("While statement : ");

                          Write the index to the screen.

                        Console.WriteLine(i);

                          Increment the variable.

                        i++;

                }

        }

}
```

Output:

```
While statement 0
While statement 1
While statement 2
While statement 3
While statement 4
While statement 5
While statement 6
While statement 7
While statement 8
While statement 9
```

A program that assigns variable in while loop:

Code:

```
using System;

class Program
{
        static void Main()
        {
                int value = 4; int i;
                // You can assign a variable in the while-loop
        condition statement.
```

```
            while ((i = value) >= 0)
            {
                // In the while-loop body, both i and value
            are equal.
                Console.WriteLine("While {0} {1}", i, value);
                value--;
            }
        }
}
```

Output:

```
While 4 4
While 3 3
While 2 2
While 1 1
While 0 0
```

Do While Loop:

It is not conventionally used much in many c# programs but still comes in handy when we want to perform certain specific operations. It is the reverse of While loop. It executes the statement for the first time compulsorily without checking the condition.

Code:

```
using System;

class Program
{
        static void Main()
        {
                int number = 0;
                 Begin do-while loop.
                 ... Terminates when number equals 2.
                do
                {
                        Console.WriteLine(number);
                                Add one to number.
                        number++;
                } while (number <= 2);
        }
}
```

Output:

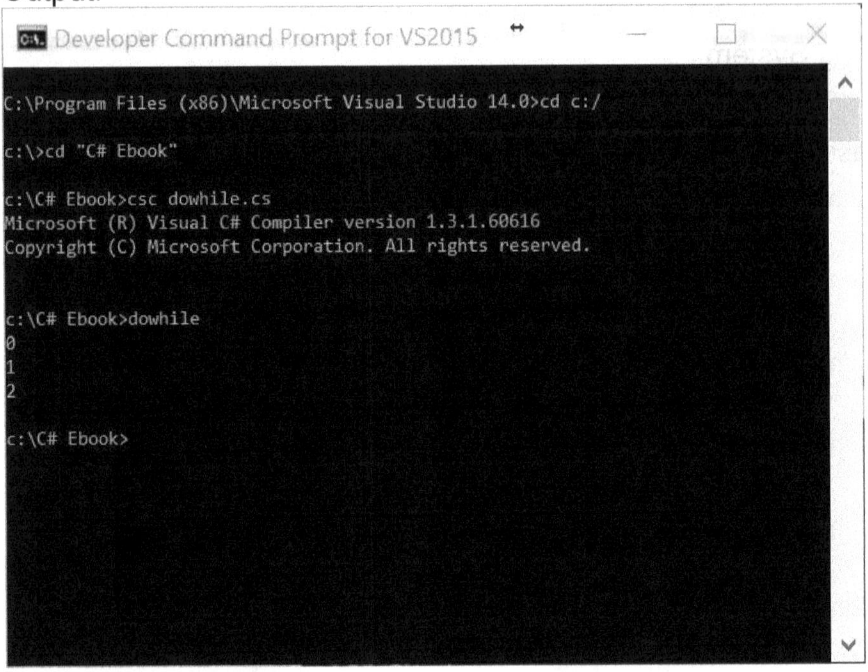
Developer Command Prompt for VS2015
C:\Program Files (x86)\Microsoft Visual Studio 14.0>cd c:/
c:\>cd "C# Ebook"
c:\C# Ebook>csc dowhile.cs
Microsoft (R) Visual C# Compiler version 1.3.1.60616
Copyright (C) Microsoft Corporation. All rights reserved.
c:\C# Ebook>dowhile
0
1
2
c:\C# Ebook>

Jump Statements:

A jump statement is used to tell a program when to deviate or take a diversion and break the flow of the loop. It comes in very handy at times.

Jump statements are of many types. Some of them are :

Break

Return

Go to

Continue

Break:

This keyword demands the program to stop execution and

continue with the next statements after the loop. Break statements are used in for, foreach and switch statements. Here we see how and where to use the break statement and it's effect.

A program explaining break statement in for and foreach loops:

Code:

```
using System;


class Program

{

        static void Main()

        {

                // Array.

                int[] array = { 5, 10, 15, 20, 25 };

                Console.WriteLine("--- for-loop and break ---");


                // Loop through indexes in the array.

                for (int i = 0; i < array.Length; i++)

                {

                        Console.WriteLine(array[i]);


                        if (array[i] == 15)

                        {

                                Console.WriteLine("Value found");
                        break;
```

```
            }
        }

        Console.WriteLine("--- foreach-loop and break ---");
    foreach (int value in array)

        {

            Console.WriteLine(value);


            if (value == 15)

            {

                Console.WriteLine("Value found");
            break;

            }

        }

    }

}
```

Output:

--- for-loop and break ---

5

10

15

Value found

--- foreach-loop and break ---

5

10

15

Value found

Program displaying effect of break on switch statement:

Code:

```
using System;

class Program
{
        static void Main()
        {
                                        for (int i = 0; i < 5; i++) // Loop
                                through five numbers.
                {
```

```
            switch (i) // Use loop index as switch
        expression.
            {
                case 0:
                case 1:
                case 2:
                    {
                        Console.WriteLine("First
                    three"); break;
                    }
                case 3:
                case 4:
                    {
                        Console.WriteLine("Last
                    two"); break;
                    }
            }
        }
    }
}
```

Output:

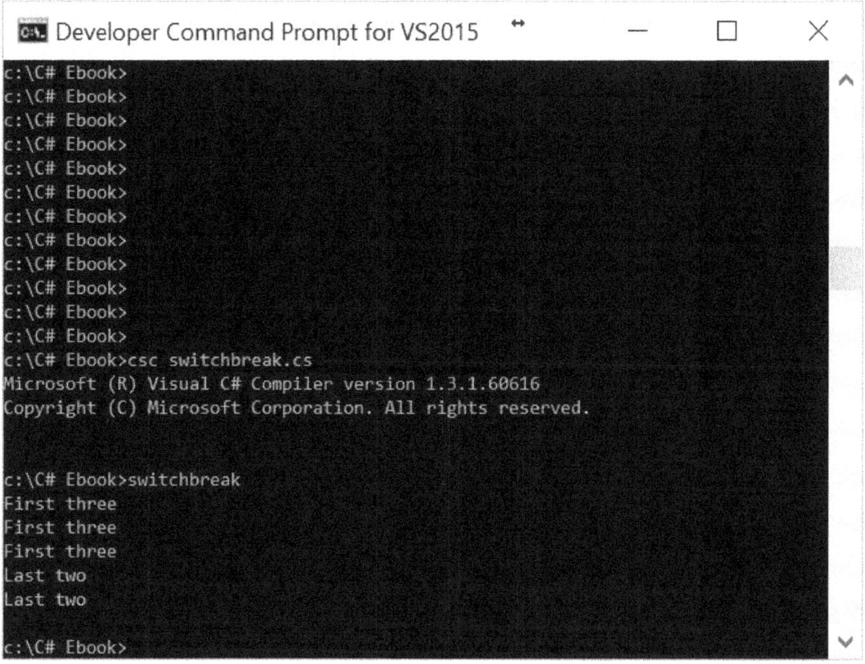
Developer Command Prompt for VS2015
c:\C# Ebook>
c:\C# Ebook>
c:\C# Ebook>
c:\C# Ebook>
c:\C# Ebook>
c:\C# Ebook>
c:\C# Ebook>
c:\C# Ebook>
c:\C# Ebook>
c:\C# Ebook>
c:\C# Ebook>
c:\C# Ebook>
c:\C# Ebook>csc switchbreak.cs
Microsoft (R) Visual C# Compiler version 1.3.1.60616
Copyright (C) Microsoft Corporation. All rights reserved.
c:\C# Ebook>switchbreak
First three
First three
First three
Last two
Last two
c:\C# Ebook>

Continue:

Continue is used to alter the flow of loop. It is used to skip the rest of the statements and continue with the flow of the loop as required.
Program displaying effect of break on switch statement:

Code:

```
using System;

using System.Threading;

class Program

{

        static void Main()
```

```
    {
        Random random = new Random();
        while (true)
        {
            // Get a random number. int value
            = random.Next();
            if ((value % 2) == 0)
            {
                continue;
            }

            if ((value % 3) == 0)
            {
                continue;
                        //2nd continue
            }
            Console.WriteLine("Not divisible by either 2
        or 3: {0}", value);
            Thread.Sleep(100);
        }
    }
}
```

Output:

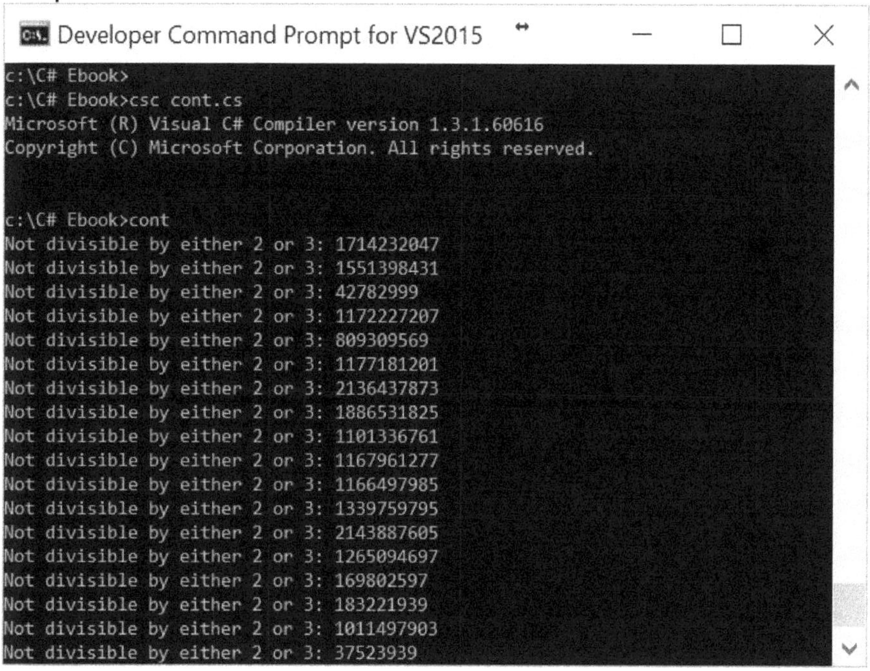

```
Developer Command Prompt for VS2015
c:\C# Ebook>
c:\C# Ebook>csc cont.cs
Microsoft (R) Visual C# Compiler version 1.3.1.60616
Copyright (C) Microsoft Corporation. All rights reserved.


c:\C# Ebook>cont
Not divisible by either 2 or 3: 1714232047
Not divisible by either 2 or 3: 1551398431
Not divisible by either 2 or 3: 42782999
Not divisible by either 2 or 3: 1172227207
Not divisible by either 2 or 3: 809309569
Not divisible by either 2 or 3: 1177181201
Not divisible by either 2 or 3: 2136437873
Not divisible by either 2 or 3: 1886531825
Not divisible by either 2 or 3: 1101336761
Not divisible by either 2 or 3: 1167961277
Not divisible by either 2 or 3: 1166497985
Not divisible by either 2 or 3: 1339759795
Not divisible by either 2 or 3: 2143887605
Not divisible by either 2 or 3: 1265094697
Not divisible by either 2 or 3: 169802597
Not divisible by either 2 or 3: 183221939
Not divisible by either 2 or 3: 1011497903
Not divisible by either 2 or 3: 37523939
```

Goto:

Goto keyword is used to transfer the flow of the program to a particularly marked label. It simply transfers the flow of program to another area where label is mentioned.

Programs:

Code:

```
using System;

class Program

{

        static void Main()

        {

                Console.WriteLine(M());
```

```
}
static int M()
{
    int dummy = 0;
    for (int a = 0; a < 10; a++)
    {
        for (int y = 0; y < 10; y++) // Run until
    condition.
        {
            for (int x = 0; x < 10; x++) // Run until
        condition.
            {
                if (x == 5 && y == 5)
                {
                    goto Outer;
                }
            }
            dummy++;
        }
    Outer:
        continue;
    }
    return dummy;
```

```
        }
}
```

Output:

50

Return:

A return statement is just a jump statement. It transfers the control to the original call area of the program.

Simply put, it is explained as in:

```
void SomeFunction() {
   int c = Add(2, 4);
}
int Add(int a, int b) {
    int total = a + b;
    return total;
}
```

Now, this return total transfers the control back to the 2nd line where the add function is called.

Module - 5 : Classes and Objects

Classes

We have been seeing the class keyword right from the start of this book in the 'Hello World' program. One can define the class in c# by using the class keyword. Once the class is defined, it can have it's own class members, function, methods, properties, indexers, events, operators, instance constructors, static constructors, destructors, and nested type declarations.

Keep a note that classes don't end with semicolon.

A simple program will clear all the doubts if any.

Code:

```
class Tiffin

{

        public void Open()

        {

                System.Console.WriteLine("Tiffin is now opened");

        }

}


class Program

{

        static void Main()

        {
                        The program starts or begins here.
```

When we want to Create a new tiffin and call the function Open on it.

Tiffin tiffin = new Tiffin();

tiffin.Open();

}

}

Output:

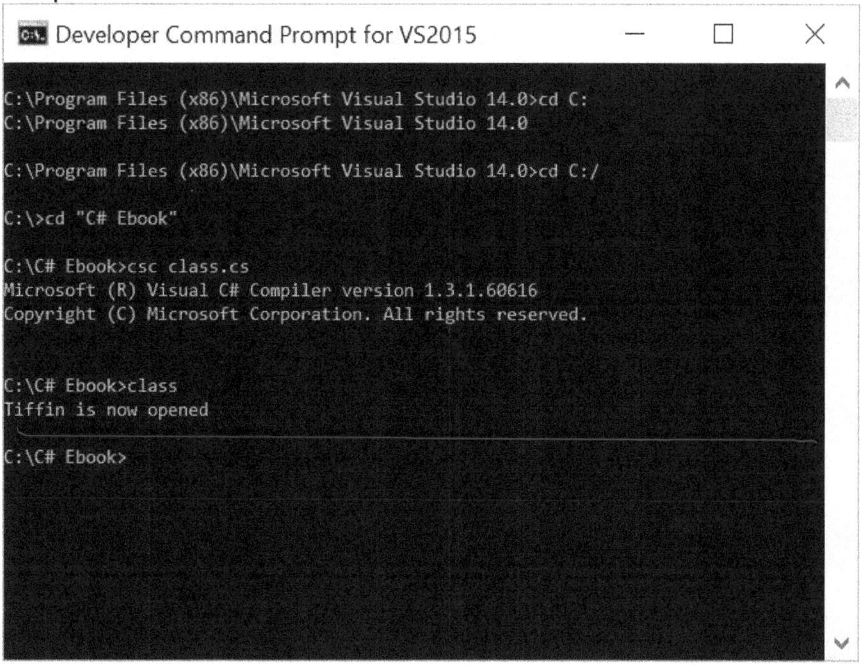
Developer Command Prompt for VS2015
C:\Program Files (x86)\Microsoft Visual Studio 14.0>cd C:
C:\Program Files (x86)\Microsoft Visual Studio 14.0
C:\Program Files (x86)\Microsoft Visual Studio 14.0>cd C:/
C:\>cd "C# Ebook"
C:\C# Ebook>csc class.cs
Microsoft (R) Visual C# Compiler version 1.3.1.60616
Copyright (C) Microsoft Corporation. All rights reserved.
C:\C# Ebook>class
Tiffin is now opened
C:\C# Ebook>

Nested Class Program:

A class declaration that occurs in other class declaration is nested class.

Code:

```
class A
{
        public int _v1;
        public class B
        {
                public int _v2;
        }
}
class Program
{
        static void Main()
        {
                A a = new
                A(); a._v1++;

                A.B ab = new A.B();
                ab._v2++;
        }
}
```

Constructor:

When a class is created, a constructor is automatically called. They usually have the same name as the class and usually initialize data members of the new object.

A simple program making widgets using constructor:

Code:

```
class Widget

{

        int _size;

        public Widget(int size)

        {

                this._size = size;

        }

}

class Program

{

        static void Main()

        {

                Widget widget1 = new Widget(10); Widget
                widget2 = new Widget(20);

        }

}
```

'This' keyword used in constructor. 'this' keyword is used when many constructors are involved and one constructor call is to be made without confusions and code bloating.

Code:

```
using System;

class Mouse

{

        public Mouse()

                : this(-1, "")

        {

                // Uses constructor initializer.

        }

        public Mouse(int weight, string name)

        {

                // Constructor implementation.
        Console.WriteLine("Constructor weight = {0}, name = {1}",

                        weight,

                        name);

        }

}

class Program

{

        static void Main()
```

```
        {
                // Test the 2 constructors for Mouse type. Mouse

                mouse1 = new Mouse();

                Mouse mouse2 = new Mouse(10, "Sam");

        }

}
```

Output:

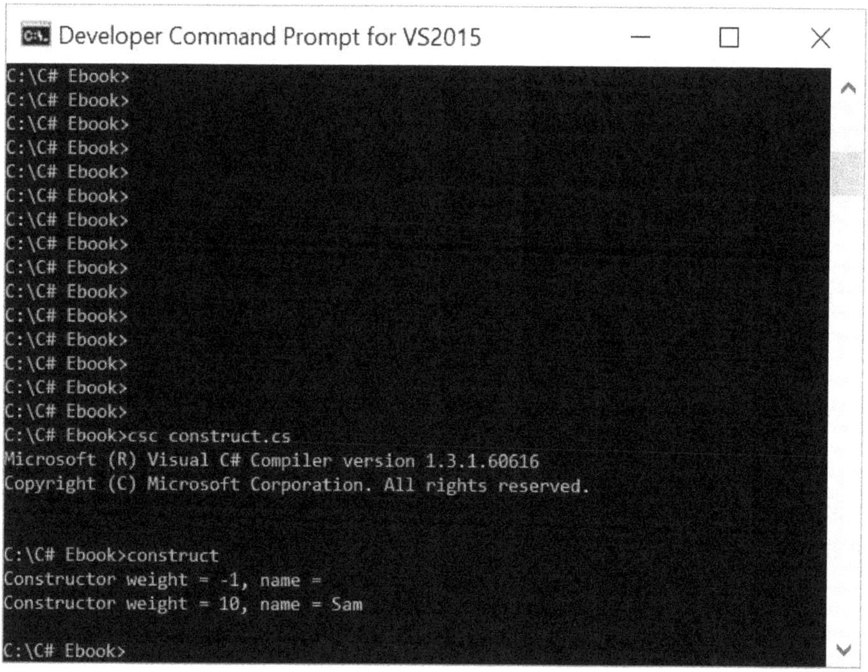
Developer Command Prompt for VS2015
C:\C# Ebook>
C:\C# Ebook>
C:\C# Ebook>
C:\C# Ebook>
C:\C# Ebook>
C:\C# Ebook>
C:\C# Ebook>
C:\C# Ebook>
C:\C# Ebook>
C:\C# Ebook>
C:\C# Ebook>
C:\C# Ebook>
C:\C# Ebook>
C:\C# Ebook>
C:\C# Ebook>
C:\C# Ebook>csc construct.cs
Microsoft (R) Visual C# Compiler version 1.3.1.60616
Copyright (C) Microsoft Corporation. All rights reserved.
C:\C# Ebook>construct
Constructor weight = -1, name =
Constructor weight = 10, name = Sam
C:\C# Ebook>

Default Constructors: Every class has a default parameterless constructor which is simple to use syntax in class declarations.

Code:

```
using System;

class Test // Has default parameterless constructor
```

```
{
        public int Value { get; set; }
}
class Program
{
        static void Main()
        {
                // Call the default constructor. Test test =
                new Test(); test.Value = 1;
                Console.WriteLine(test != null);
        }
}
```

Output:

True

Public Constructor: It allows a class to be initiated from an external location in the given program. They are used to create the instances from outside the given class.

Code:

```
using System;

class Test

{

        public Test(int a)

        {

                if (a == 0)

                {

                        throw new ArgumentException("Error", "a");

                }

        }

}

class Program
{

        static void Main()

        {

                Test test = new Test(5);

        }

}
```

Output:

//A class is instantiated.

Private Constructor: A private constructor is one which cannot be externally called. It is used to produce high quality and highly secure code. It uses the keyword private.

Code:

```
using System;

public sealed class Test

{

        public static readonly Test Instance = new Test();

        public int A;

        private Test() // This is the private constructor.

        {

                this.A = 5;

        }

}

class Program

{

        static void Main()

        {

                Test test = Test.Instance;
```

```
            // Use the class instance.

            Console.WriteLine(test.A);

            test.A++;

            Console.WriteLine(test.A);

      }

}
```

Output:

5

6

Destructor: There is automatic garbage collection in C#. We do not need to specially empty the values. It is automatically taken care of. It is executed after a class is unreachable for a long time. If we want to explicitly call, the destructor is named as started with the sign '~' (tilde).

Code:

```
using System;

class Example

{

      public Example()

      {

            Console.WriteLine("Constructor");

      }
```

```
        ~Example()
        {
                Console.WriteLine("Destructor");
        }
}
class Program
{
        static void Main()
        {
                Example x = new Example();
        }
}
```

Output:

Constructor

Destructor

Objects

Any C# type can be used as an object. Each class is derived from the base class object. Each reference is both an object and its derived types.

Simple syntax :

```
using System; using

System.Text;

class Program

{

        static void Main()

        {

                // Use an object reference. object val = new
                StringBuilder();

                Console.WriteLine(val.GetType());

        }

}
```

A Simple C# program explaining methods and encapsulation :

Code:

```
using System;

namespace BoxApplication

{
```

```
class Box
{
        Private double lengt;        // Length measures of a box
        private double breadth;   // Breadth measures of a box
        private double height;     // Height measures of a box
        public void setLength( double len )
        {
                length = len;
        }

        public void setBreadth( double bre )
        {
                breadth = bre;
        }

        public void setHeight( double hei )
        {
                height = hei;
        }
        public double getVolume()
```

```
        {
                return length * breadth * height;
        }
}
class Boxtester
{
        static void Main(string[] args)
        {
                Box Box1 = new Box();
                Box Box2 = new Box(); double
                volume;

                        Declare Box2 of type Box
                        box 1 specification
                Box1.setLength(6.0);
                Box1.setBreadth(7.0);
                Box1.setHeight(5.0);

                // box 2 specification
                Box2.setLength(12.0);
                Box2.setBreadth(13.0);
```

```
            Box2.setHeight(10.0);

            // volume of box 1

            volume = Box1.getVolume();
        Console.WriteLine("Volume of Box1 : {0}" ,volume);

            // volume of box 2

            volume = Box2.getVolume();
        Console.WriteLine("Volume of Box2 : {0}", volume);

            Console.ReadKey();

        }

    }

}
```

Output:

```
Volume of Box1 : 210

Volume of Box2 : 1560
```

Program Usage of Object type as argument:

Code:

```
using System;

class Program

{

        static void Main()

        {

                // Use string type as object. string

                value = "C# Ebook"; Test(value);

                Test((object)value);


                int number = 100;

                Test(number);

                Test((object)number);

                Test(null);

        }

        static void Test(object value)

        {
```

```
            // Test the object.

            Console.WriteLine(value != null); if (value is string)

            {

                    Console.WriteLine("String value: {0}",
            value);

            }

            else if (value is int)

            {

                    Console.WriteLine("Int value: {0}", value);

            }

        }

}
```

Output:

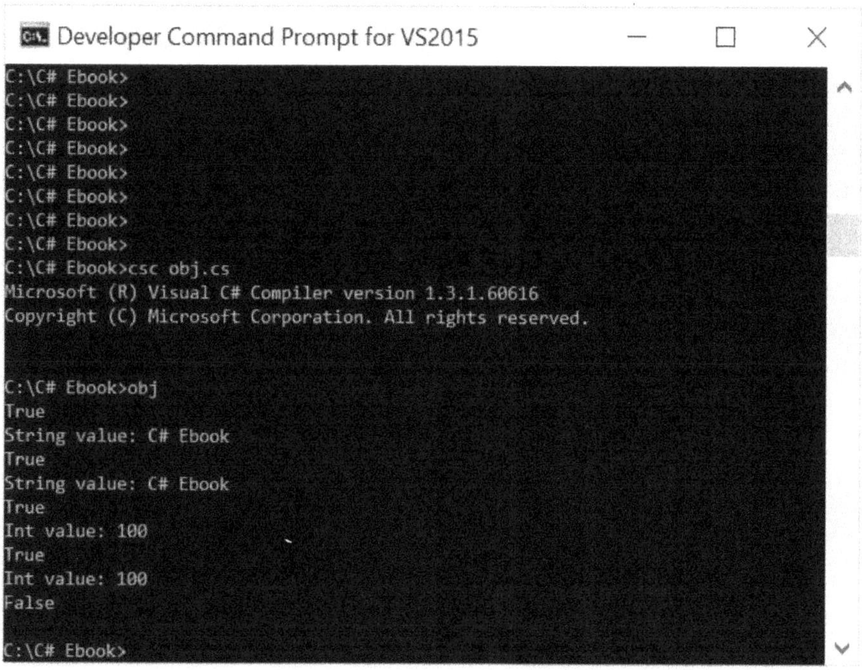
Developer Command Prompt for VS2015
C:\C# Ebook>
C:\C# Ebook>
C:\C# Ebook>
C:\C# Ebook>
C:\C# Ebook>
C:\C# Ebook>
C:\C# Ebook>
C:\C# Ebook>
C:\C# Ebook>csc obj.cs
Microsoft (R) Visual C# Compiler version 1.3.1.60616
Copyright (C) Microsoft Corporation. All rights reserved.
C:\C# Ebook>obj
True
String value: C# Ebook
True
String value: C# Ebook
True
Int value: 100
True
Int value: 100
False
C:\C# Ebook>

Inheritance

Inheritance is one of the most important factor in object oriented programming. Inheritance is the main thing that allows us to define a class in another class and makes it easy for the application. It is considered to be the optimal way and speed efficient in using inheritance.Code reusability is also increased highly by using inheritance.

With the help of inheritance, a new class can inherit all the members of the base class. The class from which it is deriving is known as the base class, while the class which is deriving is known as the derived class.

Syntax:

```
<acessspecifier> class <base_class>
{
...

}
class <derived_class> : <base_class>

{
...

}
```

Simple shape class inheriting from the base class is shown below:

Code:

```
using System;

namespace InheritanceApplication

{

        class Shape
```

```
{
        public void setWidth(int w)
        {
                width = w;
        }
        public void setHeight(int h)
        {
                height = h;
        }
        protected int width;
        protected int height;
}

// Derived class class
Rectangle: Shape
{
        public int getArea()
        {
                return (width * height);
        }
}
class RectangleTester
```

```
    {
        static void Main(string[] args)
        {
            Rectangle Rect = new Rectangle();
            Rect.setWidth(5);
            Rect.setHeight(7);

            // Print the area of the object.
        Console.WriteLine("Total area: {0}",
            Rect.getArea()); Console.ReadKey();
        }
    }
}
```

Output:

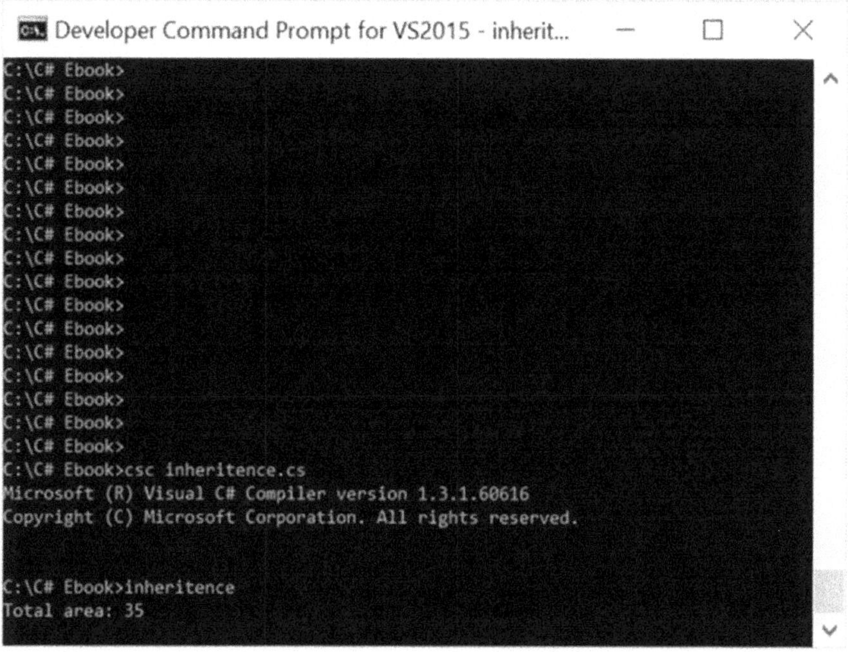
Developer Command Prompt for VS2015 - inherit...
C:\C# Ebook>
C:\C# Ebook>
C:\C# Ebook>
C:\C# Ebook>
C:\C# Ebook>
C:\C# Ebook>
C:\C# Ebook>
C:\C# Ebook>
C:\C# Ebook>
C:\C# Ebook>
C:\C# Ebook>
C:\C# Ebook>
C:\C# Ebook>
C:\C# Ebook>
C:\C# Ebook>
C:\C# Ebook>
C:\C# Ebook>
C:\C# Ebook>csc inheritence.cs
Microsoft (R) Visual C# Compiler version 1.3.1.60616
Copyright (C) Microsoft Corporation. All rights reserved.
C:\C# Ebook>inheritence
Total area: 35

Inheritance code using base class and virtual method

Code:

```
using System;

using System.Collections.Generic;

class Net

{

        public virtual void Act()

        {

        }

}
```

```
class Perl : Net
{
        public override void Act()
        {
                Console.WriteLine("Perl.Act");
        }
}
class Python : Net
{
        public override void Act()
        {
                Console.WriteLine("Python.Act");
        }
}
class Program
{
        static void Main()
        {
                List<Net> nets = new List<Net>();
                nets.Add(new Perl());
                nets.Add(new Python()); foreach
```

```
        (Net net in nets)
        {
            net.Act();
        }
    }
}
```

Output:

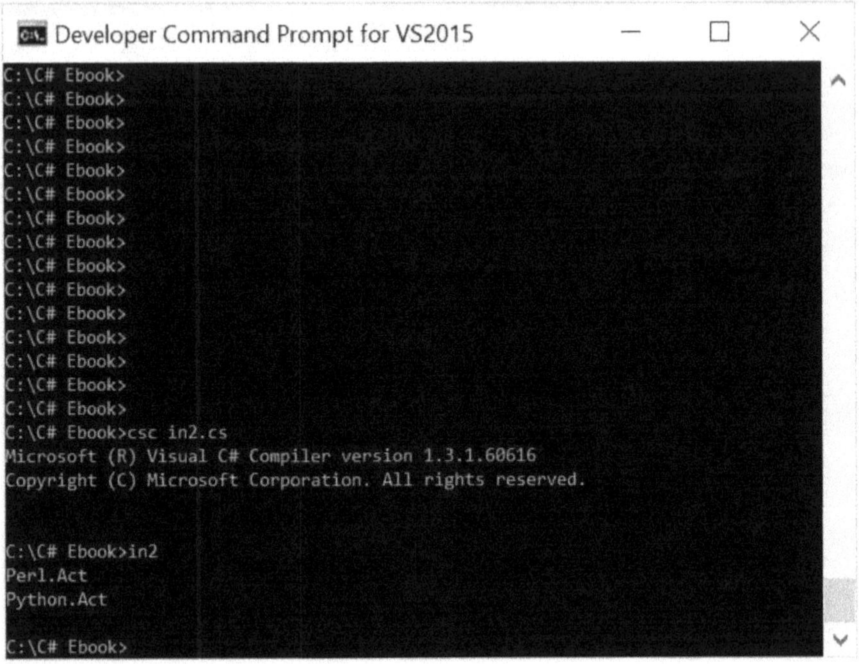
Developer Command Prompt for VS2015
C:\C# Ebook>
C:\C# Ebook>
C:\C# Ebook>
C:\C# Ebook>
C:\C# Ebook>
C:\C# Ebook>
C:\C# Ebook>
C:\C# Ebook>
C:\C# Ebook>
C:\C# Ebook>
C:\C# Ebook>
C:\C# Ebook>
C:\C# Ebook>
C:\C# Ebook>
C:\C# Ebook>
C:\C# Ebook>csc in2.cs
Microsoft (R) Visual C# Compiler version 1.3.1.60616
Copyright (C) Microsoft Corporation. All rights reserved.
C:\C# Ebook>in2
Perl.Act
Python.Act
C:\C# Ebook>

Multiple Inheritance:

Code:

```
using System;
namespace InheritanceApplication
{
    class Shape
    {
        public void setWidth(int w)
        {
            width = w;
```

```
        }
        public void setHeight(int h)
        {
                height = h;
        }
        protected int width;
        protected int height;
}
// Base class
public interface PaintCost
{
        int getCost(int area);

}
        // Derived
class Rectangle : Shape, PaintCost
{
        public int getArea()
        {
                return (width * height);
        }
        public int getCost(int area)
        {
                return area * 70;
```

```
            }
        }
        class RectangleTester
        {
            static void Main(string[] args)
            {
                Rectangle Rect = new Rectangle(); int area;
                Rect.setWidth(5);
                Rect.setHeight(7);
                area = Rect.getArea();
                Console.WriteLine("Total area is: {0}",
            Rect.getArea());
                Console.WriteLine("Total paint cost will be:
            ${0}" , Rect.getCost(area));
                Console.ReadKey();
            }
        }
    }
```

Output:

```
Developer Command Prompt for VS2015 - mulinh...
C:\C# Ebook>
C:\C# Ebook>
C:\C# Ebook>
C:\C# Ebook>
C:\C# Ebook>
C:\C# Ebook>
C:\C# Ebook>
C:\C# Ebook>
C:\C# Ebook>
C:\C# Ebook>
C:\C# Ebook>
C:\C# Ebook>
C:\C# Ebook>
C:\C# Ebook>
C:\C# Ebook>
C:\C# Ebook>
C:\C# Ebook>csc mulinheri.cs
Microsoft (R) Visual C# Compiler version 1.3.1.60616
Copyright (C) Microsoft Corporation. All rights reserved.


C:\C# Ebook>mulinheri
Total area is: 35
Total paint cost will be: $2450
```

Polymorphism

Polymorphism literally means many forms. In object oriented paradigm, it means - 'one interface many functions'

Polymorphism can be categorised in two different types:

Static Polymorphism

Dynamic Polymorphism

Static Polymorphism:

In static polymorphism, the reply to the function is done at compile time. There are two techniques of static polymorphism:

Operator Overloading

Function Overloading

Operator overloading is further discussed in the next modules.

Function Overloading:

Function overloading is a polymorphism where you can have different meaning for the same function name. The example given below uses function overloading by overloading the print() function to print various different types:

Code:

```
using System;

namespace PolymorphismApplication

{

        class Printdata

        {
```

```
void print(int i)

{

        Console.WriteLine("Printing the int: {0}", i );

}

void print(double f)

{

        Console.WriteLine("Printing the float: {0}" ,
f);

}

void print(string s)

{

        Console.WriteLine("Printing the string: {0}",
s);

}

static void Main(string[] args)

{

        Printdata p = new Printdata();

                Call print to print integer p.print(5);

                Call print to print float

        p.print(500.263);
```

```
                // Call print to print string
                p.print("Hello C++");
                Console.ReadKey();
            }
        }
}
```

Output:

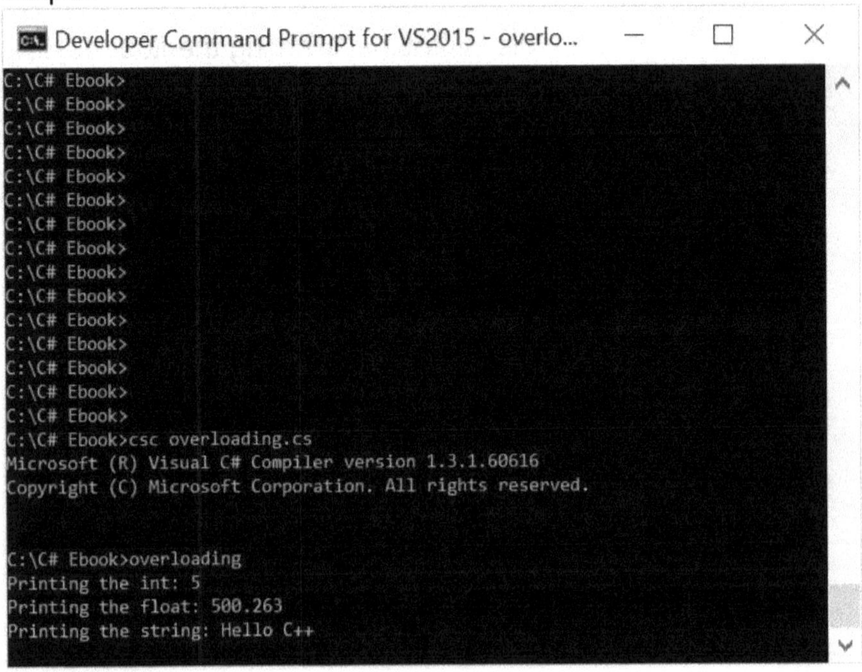
Developer Command Prompt for VS2015 - overlo...
C:\C# Ebook>
C:\C# Ebook>
C:\C# Ebook>
C:\C# Ebook>
C:\C# Ebook>
C:\C# Ebook>
C:\C# Ebook>
C:\C# Ebook>
C:\C# Ebook>
C:\C# Ebook>
C:\C# Ebook>
C:\C# Ebook>
C:\C# Ebook>
C:\C# Ebook>
C:\C# Ebook>
C:\C# Ebook>csc overloading.cs
Microsoft (R) Visual C# Compiler version 1.3.1.60616
Copyright (C) Microsoft Corporation. All rights reserved.
C:\C# Ebook>overloading
Printing the int: 5
Printing the float: 500.263
Printing the string: Hello C++

Dynamic Polymorphism:

In dynamic polymorphism, a reply to a function is determined at run-time. In dynamic polymorphism, abstract classes are used which contains the abstract methods. The derived class have more specific functionality here.

Code:

```
using System;

namespace PolymorphismApplication

{

    abstract class Shape

    {

        public abstract int area();

    }

    class Rectangle:    Shape

    {

        private int length;

        private int width;

        public Rectangle( int a=0, int b=0)

        {

            length = a;

            width = b;

        }

        public override int area ()

        {

            Console.WriteLine("Rectangle class area :");
```

```
                    return (width * length);
                }
            }

            class RectangleTester
            {
                static void Main(string[] args)
                {
                    Rectangle r = new Rectangle(10, 7); double
                a
                    = r.area(); Console.WriteLine("Area: {0}",a);
                     Console.ReadKey();
                }
            }
}
```

Output:

Rectangle class area :

Area: 70

A Sample example with code:

A dynamic polymorphism with virtual function and abstract classes is mentioned in the below program:

Code:

```
using System;

namespace PolymorphismApplication

{

        class Shapestry

        {

                protected int width, height;

                public Shapestry( int a=0, int b=0)

                {

                        width = a;

                        height = b;

                }

                public virtual int area()

                {

                        Console.WriteLine("Parent class area :");
                return 0;

                }

        }
        class Rectangle: Shapestry
```

```
{
        public Rectangle( int a=0, int b=0): base(a, b)
        {}
        public override int area ()
        {
                Console.WriteLine("Rectangle class area :");
        return (width * height);
        }
}
class Triangle: Shapestry
{
        public Triangle(int a = 0, int b = 0): base(a, b)
        {}
        public override int area()
        {
                Console.WriteLine("Triangle class area :");
        return (width * height / 2);
        }
}
class Caller
{
        public void CallArea(Shapestry sh)
        {
```

```
                int a;

                a = sh.area(); Console.WriteLine("Area: {0}",
          a);

          }

     }

     class Tester

     {

          static void Main(string[] args)

          {

                Caller c = new Caller();

                Rectangle r = new Rectangle(10, 7);
          Triangle t

                = new Triangle(10, 5);

                c.CallArea(r);   c.CallArea(t);
          Console.ReadKey();


          }

     }

}
```

Output:

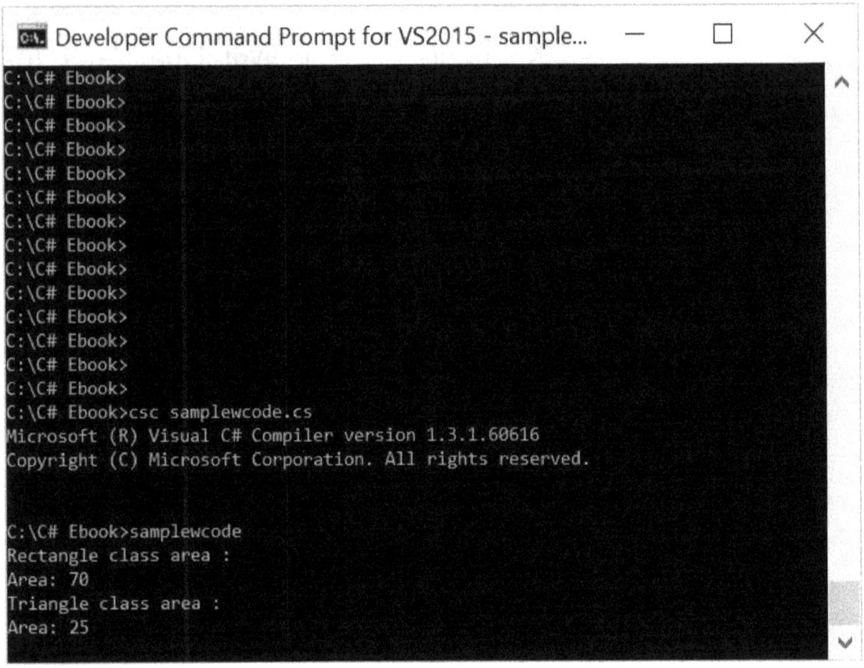
Developer Command Prompt for VS2015 - sample...
C:\C# Ebook>
C:\C# Ebook>
C:\C# Ebook>
C:\C# Ebook>
C:\C# Ebook>
C:\C# Ebook>
C:\C# Ebook>
C:\C# Ebook>
C:\C# Ebook>
C:\C# Ebook>
C:\C# Ebook>
C:\C# Ebook>
C:\C# Ebook>
C:\C# Ebook>
C:\C# Ebook>csc samplewcode.cs
Microsoft (R) Visual C# Compiler version 1.3.1.60616
Copyright (C) Microsoft Corporation. All rights reserved.
C:\C# Ebook>samplewcode
Rectangle class area :
Area: 70
Triangle class area :
Area: 25

Module - 6 : Exception Handling

There can be errors in any of the statements. Checking for each and every error in all the statements can be tiresome. We have exception handling for that. With the help of exception handling, parts of our programs can be handled for any known errors and also, specific errors can be targeted for minimal memory footprint.

We can throw any exception in the program by using the 'throw' keyword, but during execution it is automatically thrown on the command line.

Try Catch Blocks

Try and Catch blocks are used in parts of program to structure out the exception handling. Using try and catch blocks are highly recommended and also a clean code is developed using them.

Code:

```
using System;


class Program

{

        static void Main()

        {

                try

                {

                        int value = 1 / int.Parse("0");
```

```
                    Console.WriteLine(value);
                }
                catch (Exception ex)
                {
                    Console.WriteLine(ex.Message);
                }
        }
}
```

Output:

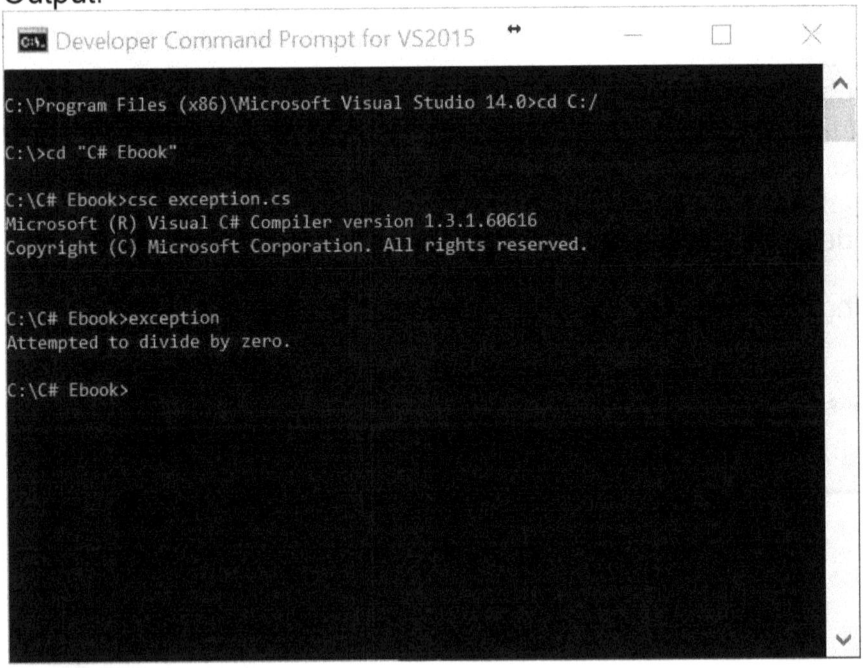
Developer Command Prompt for VS2015
C:\Program Files (x86)\Microsoft Visual Studio 14.0>cd C:/
C:\>cd "C# Ebook"
C:\C# Ebook>csc exception.cs
Microsoft (R) Visual C# Compiler version 1.3.1.60616
Copyright (C) Microsoft Corporation. All rights reserved.
C:\C# Ebook>exception
Attempted to divide by zero.
C:\C# Ebook>

Properties

There are various exception properties that can be helpful. Here, we describe a divide by zero exception and apply the following properties:

HelpLink
Message
Source
StackTrace
TargetSite

Code:

```
using System;

class Program

{

        static void Main()

        {

                try

                {

                        int value = 1 / int.Parse("0");

                }

                catch (Exception ex)

                {

                        Console.WriteLine("HelpLink = {0}", ex.HelpLink);
                        Console.WriteLine("Message = {0}", ex.Message);
                        Console.WriteLine("Source = {0}", ex.Source);
                        Console.WriteLine("StackTrace = {0}",
                        ex.StackTrace);
                        Console.WriteLine("TargetSite = {0}", ex.TargetSite);
                }

        }

}
```

Output:

```
HelpLink =

Message = Attempted to divide by zero. Source =
ConsoleApplication1
StackTrace = at Program.Main() in C:\...\Program.cs:line 9
TargetSite = Void Main()
```

DivideByZero Exception Program using try statement:

Code:

```
using System;

class Program

{

        static void Main()

        {

                        A();   B();

        }

        static void A()

        {

                try

                {

                        int value = 1 / int.Parse("0");

                }
```

```
            catch
            {
                Console.WriteLine("A");
            }
        }
        static void B()
        {
            int value = 1 / int.Parse("0");
            Console.WriteLine("B");
        }
}
```

Output:

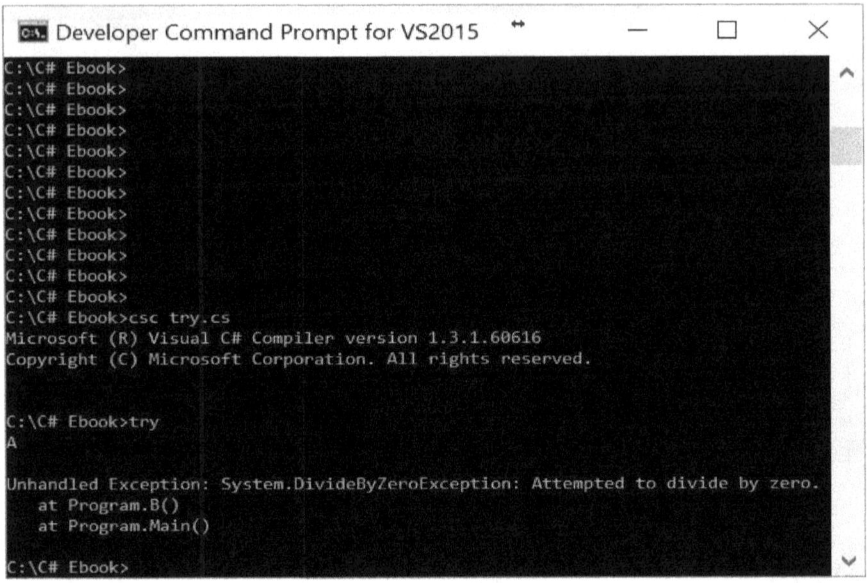
Developer Command Prompt for VS2015
C:\C# Ebook>
C:\C# Ebook>
C:\C# Ebook>
C:\C# Ebook>
C:\C# Ebook>
C:\C# Ebook>
C:\C# Ebook>
C:\C# Ebook>
C:\C# Ebook>
C:\C# Ebook>
C:\C# Ebook>
C:\C# Ebook>
C:\C# Ebook>csc try.cs
Microsoft (R) Visual C# Compiler version 1.3.1.60616
Copyright (C) Microsoft Corporation. All rights reserved.
C:\C# Ebook>try
A
Unhandled Exception: System.DivideByZeroException: Attempted to divide by zero.
at Program.B()
at Program.Main()
C:\C# Ebook>

Try with finally. Finally keyword is explained in the subsequent topics:

Code:

```
using System;

class Program

{

        static void Main()

        {

                try

                {

                        Console.WriteLine("A");

                }
```

```
            finally
            {
                    Console.WriteLine("B");
            }
        }
}
```

Output:

A

B

Catch Block

Catching an exception is done using the ‘catch’ keyword. Multiple catch blocks can be created for specific functionalities and various filters can also be used. There can also be an optional catch variable in the parenthesis after the keyword

Code:

```
using System;

class Program
{
    static void Main()
    {
        // You can use an empty catch block. try
        {
            DivideByZero();
        }
        catch
        {
            Console.WriteLine("0");
        }
        // You can specify a variable in the catch. try
        {
            DivideByZero();
        }
        catch (Exception ex)
```

```
        {
                Console.WriteLine("1");
        }
        // You can use multiple catch blocks. try
        {
                DivideByZero();
        }
        catch (DivideByZeroException)
        {
                Console.WriteLine("2");
        }
        catch
        {
                Console.WriteLine("3");
        }
}
static int DivideByZero()
{
        int value1 = 1;
        int value2 = int.Parse("0"); return
        value1 / value2;
```

```
        }
}
```

Output:

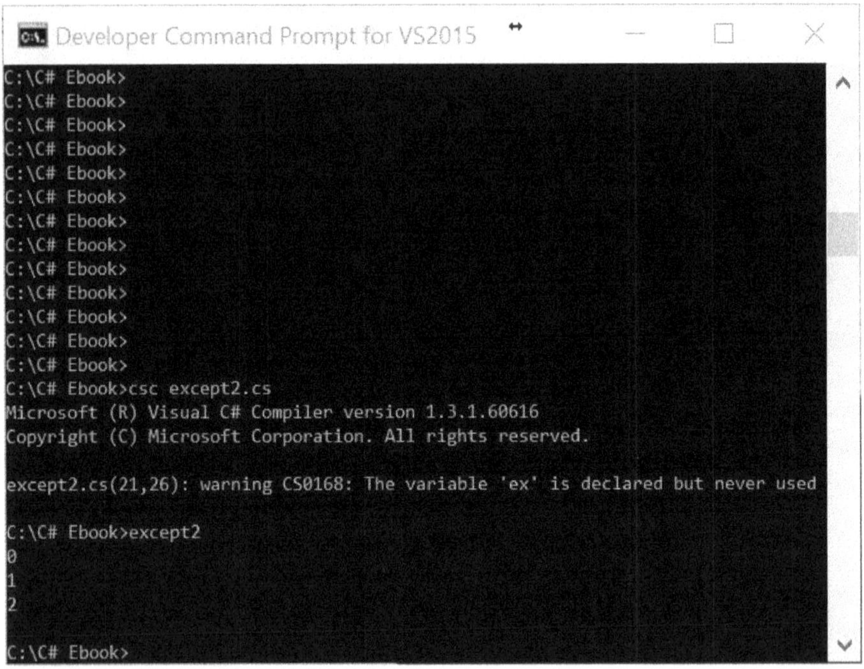
Developer Command Prompt for VS2015
C:\C# Ebook>
C:\C# Ebook>
C:\C# Ebook>
C:\C# Ebook>
C:\C# Ebook>
C:\C# Ebook>
C:\C# Ebook>
C:\C# Ebook>
C:\C# Ebook>
C:\C# Ebook>
C:\C# Ebook>
C:\C# Ebook>
C:\C# Ebook>
C:\C# Ebook>csc except2.cs
Microsoft (R) Visual C# Compiler version 1.3.1.60616
Copyright (C) Microsoft Corporation. All rights reserved.
except2.cs(21,26): warning CS0168: The variable 'ex' is declared but never used
C:\C# Ebook>except2
0
1
2
C:\C# Ebook>

C# program using catch, when and filter exceptions:

Code:

```
using System;
class Program
{
        static void Main()
        {
                try
```

```
            {
                  throw new ArgumentException("Invalid x
            argument");
            }
            catch (ArgumentException ex) when (ex.Message
      == "Invalid x argument")
            {
                  // This is reached. Console.WriteLine("X");
            }
            catch (ArgumentException ex) when (ex.Message
      == "Invalid y argument")
            {
                  This is not reached.
                  ... Change the string to have "y" and it will
be reached.
                  Console.WriteLine("Y");
            }
      }
}
```

Output:

X

Finally and Throw Blocks

Finally block is an essential part of the exception handling process. Whatever is stated in the finally block is always executed, no matter what the exception is (if any). Finally block is called irrespective of whether any errors or exception is called.

Finally block ensure that some logic is executed before terminating the loop

Program that controls flow and uses Finally block:

Code:

```
using System;


class Program

{

        static void Main()

        {

                try

                {

                        Get random integer for use in the control of
flow.

                        If the number is 0, an error will occur.

                        If the number is 1, the method returns.

                        Otherwise, fall through to the end.

                        int random = new Random().Next(0, 3); // 0,
                1, 2
```

```
                if (random == 0)
                {
                    throw new Exception("Random = 0");
                }
                if (random == 1)
                {
                    Console.WriteLine("Random = 1");
                return;

                }
                Console.WriteLine("Random = 2");
            }
            finally
            {
                // This the statement is executed before
            Main method exits.
                It is reached when an exception is thrown.
                Also, It is reached after the return
            statement.
                and also It is reached in other cases too.
                Console.WriteLine("Control flow reaches
            finally block");
            }
        }
}
```

Output:

Possible output #1

Unhandled Exception: System.Exception: Random = 0 at Program.Main() ...
Control flow reaches finally

Possible output #2
Random = 1
Control flow reaches finally

Possible output #3
Random = 2
Control flow reaches finally

Throw Block

Throw keyword is used to create and throw exceptions in c#. We can throw a different exception that the one caught in catch block with the help of thies block

Code:

```
using System;


class Program

{

        static void Main()

        {

                // Comment out the first 1-2 method invocations. try

                {

                        A();
```

```
            B();
            C(null);
        }
        catch (Exception ex)
        {
            Console.WriteLine(ex);
        }
}

static void A()
{
        // Rethrow syntax. try
        {
            int value = 1 / int.Parse("0");
        }
        catch
        {
            throw;
        }
}
static void B()
```

```
{
    // Filtering exception types. try
    {
        int value = 1 / int.Parse("0");
    }
    catch (DivideByZeroException ex)
    {
        throw ex;
    }
}

static void C(string value)
{
    // Generate new exception. if
    (value == null)
    {
        throw new ArgumentNullException("value");
    }
}
}
```

Output:

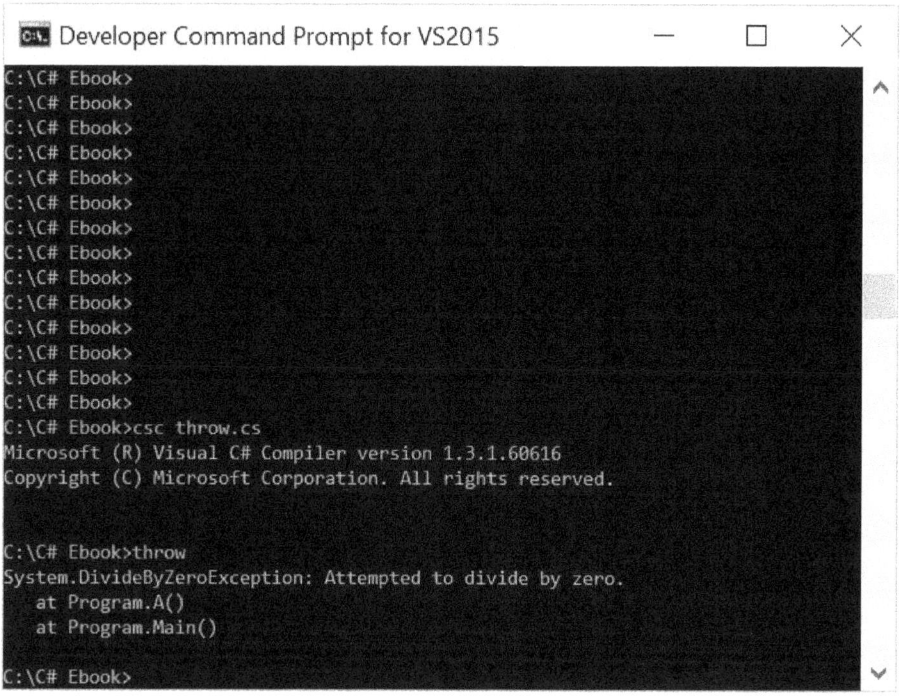
Developer Command Prompt for VS2015
C:\C# Ebook>
C:\C# Ebook>
C:\C# Ebook>
C:\C# Ebook>
C:\C# Ebook>
C:\C# Ebook>
C:\C# Ebook>
C:\C# Ebook>
C:\C# Ebook>
C:\C# Ebook>
C:\C# Ebook>
C:\C# Ebook>
C:\C# Ebook>
C:\C# Ebook>
C:\C# Ebook>csc throw.cs
Microsoft (R) Visual C# Compiler version 1.3.1.60616
Copyright (C) Microsoft Corporation. All rights reserved.
C:\C# Ebook>throw
System.DivideByZeroException: Attempted to divide by zero.
at Program.A()
at Program.Main()
C:\C# Ebook>

Program showing rethrows:

Code:

```
using System;

class Program

{

        static void Main()

        {

                try

                {

                        X();
```

```
        }
        catch (Exception ex)
        {
            Console.WriteLine(ex.TargetSite);
        }
        try
        {
            Y();
        }
        catch (Exception ex)
        {
            Console.WriteLine(ex.TargetSite);
        }
    }
    static void X()
    {
        try
        {
            int.Parse("?");
        }
        catch (Exception)
```

```
            {
                throw; // [Rethrow construct]
            }
        }
        static void Y()
        {
            try
            {
                int.Parse("?");
            }
            catch (Exception ex)
            {
                throw ex; // [Throw captured ex variable]
            }
        }
}
```

Output:

Void StringToNumber(System.String, ...)
Void Y()

Throw is usually used as a statement but sometimes, it is also used as in an expression. The below program uses throw as in an expression.

Code:

```
using System;

class Program

{

    static void Test(string argument)

    {

        Use null coalescing operator with throw expression.

        ... If argument is null, throw.

        var value = argument ?? throw new ArgumentException("Bad argument");

        Console.WriteLine("HERE");

    }

    static void Main()

    {

        Test("bird");

        Test(null);

    }

}
```

Output:

HERE

Unhandled Exception: System.ArgumentException: Bad argument at Program.Test(String argument) in c:\users\...Program.cs:line 9 at Program.Main() in c:\users\...Program.cs:line 16

Throw Expression in ternary:

Code:

```
using System;
class Program

{

        static void Main()

        {

                string test = "bird";

                 Throw can be used in ternary. char tenth =
                test.Length >= 10 ?
                        test[9] :
                        throw new Exception("Not ten characters");
                        Not reached.
                Console.WriteLine(tenth);

        }

}
```

Output:

Unhandled Exception: System.Exception: Not ten characters at Program.Main() in c:\users\...Program.cs:line 9

User Defined Exceptions

In C# we can create our own user defined exceptions that can handle the flow and errors the way we want it. It can be used to display meaningful error messages rather than the conventional error stack print.

Code:

```
using System;

public class InvalidAgedException : Exception

{

        public InvalidAgedException(String message)

                : base(message)

        {


        }

}

public class TestUserDefinedException

{

        static void validate(int age)

        {

                if (age < 18)

                {

                        throw new InvalidAgedException("Sorry,
                Your age must be greater than 18");
```

```
        }
    }
    public static void Main(string[] args)
    {
        try
        {
            validate(12);
        }
        catch (InvalidAgedException e) {
        Console.WriteLine(e); }

        Console.WriteLine("Execution of Rest of the
    code");
    }
}
```

Output:

InvalidAgeException: Sorry, Your age must be greater than 18
Rest of the code

Module - 7 : Mega Project

C# is one of the main languages used for a Window-Based Application. As such it seems only fitting to include an example of a Window-based application in this book. However, some window-based application can be vast and complex making it out of scope for this introductory level book. It is possible, though, to introduce the basic elements common to all applications. Further, these elements can be combined into a minimal Windows application skeleton that forms the foundation for our Window-based application.

Now, we are all set to go guns blazing to understand how to write a basic calculator application. We have learnt all the basics of object oriented programming, right from functions, and it's methods to exception handling. It is that time where you try this application on your own and make it count. Do not get overwhelmed by the number of lines of code. It's very simple if you break it into pieces and try to understand.

Note: You will require an IDE to perform and execute this code. I recommend using Visual Studio as it is the Microsoft's official Integrated Development Environment(IDE).

Scienti c Calculator App

Step 1:

Import Statements. If you are using an IDE, you do not need to worry about this, as this is already taken care of. All the import statements are added as and when necessary by the IDE itself. Just for the reference we will need these libraries, and hence imported.

```
using System;
using System.Collections.Generic;
using System.ComponentModel;
using System.Data;
using System.Drawing;
using System.Linq;
using System.Text;
using System.Threading.Tasks;
using System.Windows.Forms;
```

Step 2:

Declaring a namespace and naming a class. Here our

1.

```
namespace SC
{
public partial class frmScientificCalculator : Form
{
```

Step 3:

Declaring all the variables. Don't worry if you don't get it all at one go, you can always add more as and when you proceed.

```
int sign = 0;

double num1;

double num2; //Declarations

int add = 0; //Addition operation

int sub = 0; //Subtraction operation

int mul = 0; //Multiplication

int div = 0; //Division

int modBit = 0; //The mode bit

Boolean fl = false;

String s, x;
```

Step 4:

Declaring the constructor:

```
public frmScientificCalculator() //The initial constructor

{

InitializeComponent();

}
```

Step 5:

Now is the task wherein you will write one function code for a button and copy for all the rest 9 buttons.

```
private void btn1_Click(object sender, EventArgs e) //Function
for button 1

{
if (sign == 0)
{
      txtInput.Text = txtInput.Text + Convert.ToString(1);
}
else if (sign == 1)
{
      txtInput.Text = Convert.ToString(1);
      sign = 0;
}
fl = true;
}

private void btn2_Click(object sender, EventArgs e) //Function
for button 2
{
if (sign == 0)
{
      txtInput.Text = txtInput.Text + Convert.ToString(2);
}
else if (sign == 1)
{
      txtInput.Text = Convert.ToString(2);
      sign = 0;
}
fl=true;
}


private void btn3_Click(object sender, EventArgs e) //Function
for button 3
{
```

```
if (sign == 0)
{
    txtInput.Text = txtInput.Text + Convert.ToString(3);
}
else if (sign == 1)
{
    txtInput.Text = Convert.ToString(3);
    sign = 0;
}
fl=true;
}
private void btn4_Click(object sender, EventArgs e) //Function for button 4
{
if (sign == 0)
{
    txtInput.Text = txtInput.Text + Convert.ToString(4);
}
else if (sign == 1)
{
    txtInput.Text = Convert.ToString(4);
    sign = 0;
}
fl=true;
}
private void btn5_Click(object sender, EventArgs e) //Function for button 5
{
if (sign == 0)
{
    txtInput.Text = txtInput.Text + Convert.ToString(5);
}
else if (sign == 1)
{
    txtInput.Text = Convert.ToString(5);
    sign = 0;
```

```
}
fl=true;
}

private void btn6_Click(object sender, EventArgs e) //Function for button 6
{
if (sign == 0)
{
    txtInput.Text = txtInput.Text + Convert.ToString(6);
}
else if (sign == 1)
{
    txtInput.Text = Convert.ToString(6);
    sign = 0;
}
fl=true;
}

private void btn7_Click(object sender, EventArgs e) //Function for button 7
{
if (sign == 0)
{
    txtInput.Text = txtInput.Text + Convert.ToString(7);
}
else if (sign == 1)
{
    txtInput.Text = Convert.ToString(7);
    sign = 0;
}
fl=true;
}

private void btn8_Click(object sender, EventArgs e) //Function for button 8
{
if (sign == 0)
```

```
{
txtInput.Text = txtInput.Text + Convert.ToString(8);
}
else if (sign == 1)
{
txtInput.Text = Convert.ToString(8);
sign = 0;
}
fl=true;
}

private void btnnine_Click(object sender, EventArgs e)
//Function for button 9
{
if (sign == 0)
{
txtInput.Text = txtInput.Text + Convert.ToString(9);
}
else if (sign == 1)
{
txtInput.Text = Convert.ToString(9);
sign = 0;
}
fl=true;
}
private void btnZero_Click(object sender, EventArgs e)
//Function for button 0
{
if (sign == 0)
{
txtInput.Text = txtInput.Text + Convert.ToString(0);
}
else if (sign == 1)
{
txtInput.Text = Convert.ToString(0);
sign = 0;
}
fl=true;
}
```

Step 6:
Do the same as in step 5, but now for method buttons such as addition, multiplication, subtraction, etc.

```
private void reset_SignBits() //Reset Button Function
{
add = 0;
sub = 0;
mul = 0;
div = 0;
modBit = 0;
fl = false;
}
private void btnAdd_Click(object sender, EventArgs e) //The Add button
{
if (txtInput.Text.Length != 0)
{
    calculate();
    reset_SignBits();
    add = 1;
    sign = 1;
}
}
private void btnMinus_Click(object sender, EventArgs e) //The Minus button
{
if (txtInput.Text.Length != 0)
{
    num2 = Convert.ToDouble(txtInput.Text);
    calculate();
    reset_SignBits();
    sub = 1;
    sign = 1;
}
```

```
}
private void btnTimes_Click(object sender, EventArgs e) //The Multiplication button

{
if (txtInput.Text.Length != 0)
{
calculate();
reset_SignBits();
mul = 1;
sign = 1;
}
}
private void btnDivide_Click(object sender, EventArgs e) //The Division button
{
if (txtInput.Text.Length != 0)
{
calculate();
reset_SignBits();
div = 1;
sign = 1;
}
}
private void btnEqual_Click(object sender, EventArgs e) //Equal To Button
{
if (txtInput.Text.Length != 0)
{
calculate();
reset_SignBits();
}
sign = 1;
}

private void btnDot_Click(object sender, EventArgs e) //Decimal Button
{
int i = 0;
```

```
char chr = '\0';
int decimal_Indicator = 0;
int l = txtInput.Text.Length¬1;
if (sign != 1)
{
    for (i = 0; i <= l; i++)
    {
            chr = txtInput.Text[i];
            if (chr == '.')
    {
                    decimal_Indicator = 1;
    }
    }

    if (decimal_Indicator != 1)
    {
            txtInput.Text = txtInput.Text +
Convert.ToString(".");
    }
}
}
private void btnsqrt_Click(object sender, EventArgs e)
//Square Root
{
double s,l;
l = Convert.ToDouble(txtInput.Text);
s = Math.Sqrt(l);
txtInput.Text = Convert.ToString(s);
}

private void btn1divx_Click(object sender, EventArgs e)
{
    txtInput.Text =        (1       /
Convert.ToDouble(txtInput.Text)).ToString(); }

private void btnxfoctorial_Click(object sender, EventArgs e)
//factorial Button
{
try
```

```
{
long fact = 1;
for (int i = 1; i <= Convert.ToInt32(txtInput.Text); i++)

{
        fact = fact * i;
}
txtInput.Text = Convert.ToString(fact);
}
catch (Exception ex)
{
MessageBox.Show(ex.Message,  "Error",
MessageBoxButtons.OK, MessageBoxIcon.Error);
}
}
private void btnLog_Click(object sender, EventArgs e) //Log
value button
{
try
{
if (txtInput.Text.Length != 0)
{
double l;
l = Math.Log(Convert.ToDouble(txtInput.Text));
txtInput.Text = Convert.ToString(l);
}
sign = 1;
}
catch (Exception ex)
{
MessageBox.Show(ex.Message,  "Error",
MessageBoxButtons.OK, MessageBoxIcon.Error);
}
}
private void btnLog10_Click(object sender, EventArgs e) //Log to
the base 10 button
{
try
{
```

```
if (txtInput.Text.Length != 0)
{
double l;
l = Math.Log10(Convert.ToDouble(txtInput.Text));
txtInput.Text = Convert.ToString(l);
}
sign = 1;
}
catch (Exception ex)
{
MessageBox.Show(ex.Message,  "Error",
MessageBoxButtons.OK, MessageBoxIcon.Error);
}
}
private void btnex_Click(object sender, EventArgs e)
//Exponential Button
{
try
{
if (txtInput.Text.Length != 0)
{
double l;
l = Math.Exp(Convert.ToDouble(txtInput.Text));
txtInput.Text = Convert.ToString(l);
}
sign = 1;
}
catch (Exception ex)
{
MessageBox.Show(ex.Message,  "Error",
MessageBoxButtons.OK, MessageBoxIcon.Error);
}
}
private void Form6_Load(object sender, EventArgs e)
{
}
```

Step 7 :

As this is a scientific calculator that we are making, we use all the trigonometry operations too:

```
private void btnSin_Click(object sender, EventArgs e)
//Trigonometry Sin
{
try
{
if (txtInput.Text.Length != 0)
{
double l;
l = Math.Sin(Convert.ToDouble(txtInput.Text));
txtInput.Text = Convert.ToString(l);
}
sign = 1;
}
catch (Exception ex)
{
MessageBox.Show(ex.Message, "Error",
MessageBoxButtons.OK, MessageBoxIcon.Error);
}
}
private void btnCos_Click(object sender, EventArgs e)
//Trigonometry Cos
{
try
{
if (txtInput.Text.Length != 0)
{
double l;
l = Math.Cos(Convert.ToDouble(txtInput.Text));
txtInput.Text = Convert.ToString(l);
}
sign = 1;
}
catch (Exception ex)
```

```
{
368.    MessageBox.Show(ex.Message,  "Error",
MessageBoxButtons.OK, MessageBoxIcon.Error);
}
}
372. private void btnTan_Click(object sender, EventArgs e)
//Trigonometry Tan
{
try
{
if (txtInput.Text.Length != 0)
{
double l;
l = Math.Tan(Convert.ToDouble(txtInput.Text));
txtInput.Text = Convert.ToString(l);
}
}
catch (Exception ex)
{
385.    MessageBox.Show(ex.Message,  "Error",
MessageBoxButtons.OK, MessageBoxIcon.Error);
}
}
```

Step 8 :

In a scientific calculator there are various accessibility options for rounding off, ceiling and flooring the value. These are optional, but the more you practice, the more good you will get at it.

```
private void btnRound_Click(object sender, EventArgs e)
//Rounding of value
{
try
{
if (txtInput.Text.Length != 0)

{
```

```
double l;
l = Math.Round(Convert.ToDouble(txtInput.Text));
txtInput.Text = Convert.ToString(l);
}
sign = 1;
}
catch (Exception ex)
{
402.   MessageBox.Show(ex.Message, "Error",
MessageBoxButtons.OK, MessageBoxIcon.Error);
}
}
private void btnFloor_Click(object sender, EventArgs e) //Floor
function
{
try
{
if (txtInput.Text.Length != 0)
{
double l;
l = Math.Floor(Convert.ToDouble(txtInput.Text));
txtInput.Text = Convert.ToString(l);
}
sign = 1;
}
catch (Exception ex)
{
420.   MessageBox.Show(ex.Message, "Error",
MessageBoxButtons.OK, MessageBoxIcon.Error);
}
}
private void btnTruncate_Click(object sender, EventArgs e)
//Truncate function
{
try
{
if (txtInput.Text.Length != 0)
{
double l;
```

```
I = Math.Truncate(Convert.ToDouble(txtInput.Text));
txtInput.Text = Convert.ToString(I);
}
sign = 1;
}
catch (Exception ex)
{
438.    MessageBox.Show(ex.Message,  "Error",
MessageBoxButtons.OK, MessageBoxIcon.Error);
}
}
442. private void btnCeil_Click(object sender, EventArgs e)
//Ceiling Function
{
try
{
if (txtInput.Text.Length != 0)
{
double I;
I = Math.Ceiling(Convert.ToDouble(txtInput.Text));
txtInput.Text = Convert.ToString(I);
}
sign = 1;
}
catch (Exception ex)
{
456.    MessageBox.Show(ex.Message,  "Error",
MessageBoxButtons.OK, MessageBoxIcon.Error);
}
}
460. private void btnInvSin_Click(object sender, EventArgs e)
//Inverse Sin
{
try
{
if (txtInput.Text.Length != 0)
{

double I;
```

```
l = Math.Asin(Convert.ToDouble(txtInput.Text));
txtInput.Text = Convert.ToString(l);
}
sign = 1;
}
catch (Exception ex)
{
474.   MessageBox.Show(ex.Message,  "Error",
MessageBoxButtons.OK, MessageBoxIcon.Error);
}
}
private void btnSinh_Click(object sender, EventArgs e) //Sinh
{
try
{
if (txtInput.Text.Length != 0)
{
double l;
l = Math.Sinh(Convert.ToDouble(txtInput.Text));
txtInput.Text = Convert.ToString(l);
}
sign = 1;
}
catch (Exception ex)
{
492.   MessageBox.Show(ex.Message,  "Error",
MessageBoxButtons.OK, MessageBoxIcon.Error);
}
}
private void btnCosh_Click(object sender, EventArgs e) //Cosh
{
try
{
if (txtInput.Text.Length != 0)
{
double l;
l = Math.Cosh(Convert.ToDouble(txtInput.Text));
txtInput.Text = Convert.ToString(l);
}
```

```
sign = 1;
}
catch (Exception ex)
{
510.   MessageBox.Show(ex.Message,  "Error",
MessageBoxButtons.OK, MessageBoxIcon.Error);
}
}
private void button24_Click(object sender, EventArgs e)
{
try
{
if (txtInput.Text.Length != 0)
{
double l;
l = Math.Tanh(Convert.ToDouble(txtInput.Text));
txtInput.Text = Convert.ToString(l);
}
sign = 1;
}
catch (Exception ex)
{
528.   MessageBox.Show(ex.Message,  "Error",
MessageBoxButtons.OK, MessageBoxIcon.Error);
}
}
private void btnInvCos_Click(object sender, EventArgs e)
//Inverse Cos
{
try
{
if (txtInput.Text.Length != 0)
{
double l;
l = Math.Acos(Convert.ToDouble(txtInput.Text));
txtInput.Text = Convert.ToString(l);
}

sign = 1;
```

```
}
catch (Exception ex)
{
546.   MessageBox.Show(ex.Message,  "Error",
MessageBoxButtons.OK, MessageBoxIcon.Error);
}
}
private void btnInvTan_Click(object sender, EventArgs e)
//Inverse Tan
{
try
{
554.   if (txtInput.Text.Length != 0)
555.   {
double l;
l = Math.Atan(Convert.ToDouble(txtInput.Text));
txtInput.Text = Convert.ToString(l);
}
sign = 1;
}
catch (Exception ex)
{
564.   MessageBox.Show(ex.Message,  "Error",
MessageBoxButtons.OK, MessageBoxIcon.Error);
}
}
```

Step 9 :

The main brains of the program. The main calculate function wherein all the programming logic is situated. Please go through and try to make it on your own to improve your cognitive skills on the go.

```
private void calculate() //The main calculate function
{
if (txtInput.Text != ".")
{
```

```
num2 = Convert.ToDouble(txtInput.Text);
if (fl == false)
{
        num1 = num2;
}
else if (add == 1)
{
        num1 = num1 + num2;
}
else if (sub == 1)
{
        num1 = num1 ¬ num2;
}
else if (mul == 1)
{
        num1 = num1 * num2;
}
else if (div == 1)
{
        num1 = num1 / num2;
}
else if (modBit == 1)
{

        num2 = Convert.ToInt32(txtInput.Text);
        num1 = Convert.ToInt32(num1 % num2);
}

else
{
        num1 = num2;
}
txtInput.Text = Convert.ToString(num1);

}
}
private void btnmod_Click(object sender, EventArgs e) //mod
button
{
```

```
if (txtInput.Text.Length != 0)
{
calculate();
reset_SignBits();
modBit = 1;
sign = 1;
}
}
private void btnPI_Click(object sender, EventArgs e) //Pi 3.14
{
txtInput.Text = Math.PI.ToString();
sign = 1;
}
private void btnCLR_Click(object sender, EventArgs e) //Clear
Button
{
txtInput.Clear();
sign = 0;
num1 = 0;
num2 = 0;
reset_SignBits();
}
private void btnbackspace_Click(object sender, EventArgs e)
{
s = txtInput.Text;
int l = s.Length;
for (int i = 0; i < l ¬ 1; i++)
{
x += s[i];
}
txtInput.Text = x;
x = "";
}
}
}
```

You must be going through a lot here, if you are just reading this rather than practically doing it. It is pretty easy if you try. I broke the code into steps so that you are encouraged enough to try it on your own. Still, if you feel like you are stuck somewhere, Please refer to the below given code:

https://www.dropbox.com/s/las3dvaqtzae9tz/Source%20Code%20%281%29.pdf?dl=0

The final display of the calculator should look something just like this:

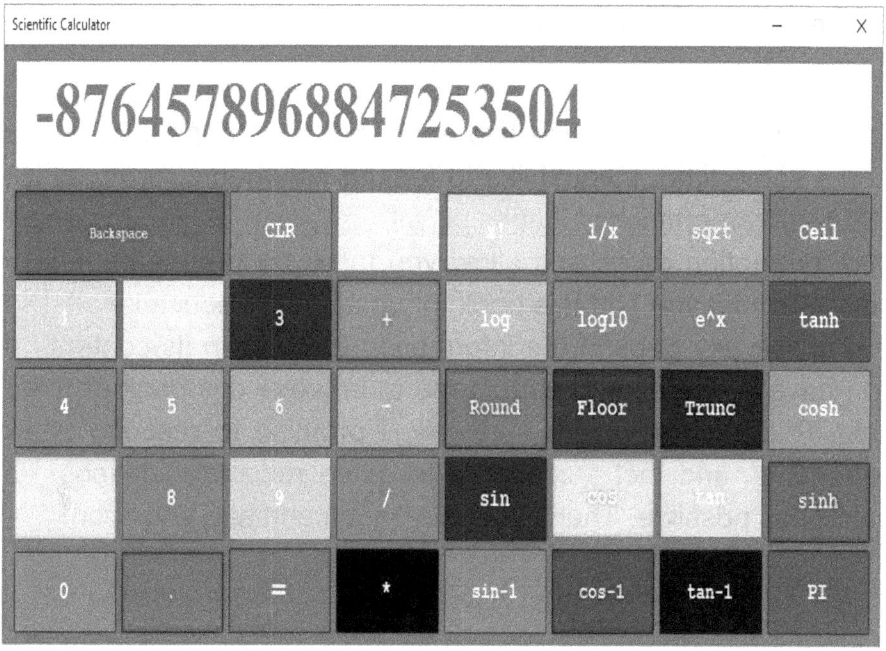

You can make it even simpler by omitting some of the functionalities. Rest is all self understood and I am sure you are going to flourish ahead in making even better applications.

Programming in C# is very easy and given proper efforts, you have the potential to get ahead in an exponential way. C# is extensively used nowadays and later to come. Please practice a lot to get a perfect hold of this programming language and use and contribute on stackover flow and other QA sites.

Signing off. Good Luck! :)

Thank you so much for reading my book, that means a lot to me. At the same time, I would like to remind you to join my email list https://williamrothschild.lpages.co/william-s-rothschild/ to benefit from promotion dates and allow you to be up to date on what I plan. Also did you find this book interesting and educational? Did you notice any gaps in the information given or in its content? If you have a proposal to enable me to improve this book and the next, PLEASE leave me a review. I promise to respond to all comments and act according to your recommendations as quickly as possible. Thank you very much and see you soon!

www.ingramcontent.com/pod-product-compliance
Lightning Source LLC
Chambersburg PA
CBHW071117050326
40690CB00008B/1247
9781548136529